Southern Counties Branch Line Steam

MICHAEL WELCH

Capital Transport

ISBN 978-1-85414-359-4

Published by
Capital Transport Publishing Ltd
www.capitaltransport.com

Printed by
1010 Printing International Ltd

Front cover: Despite its close proximity to London the Horsham to Guildford line was a true backwater. Apart from Cranleigh, it served no intermediate settlements of any consequence and in the spring the number of daily visitors to Baynards to admire the station's display of dahlias probably exceeded the number of passengers. The scheduled passenger service remained a stronghold of steam until the end, Ivatt 2-6-2Ts being staple motive power supplemented by Q1 Class locomotives from Guildford shed. Here, No.41301 is seen leaving Rudgwick with the 10.34am Guildford to Horsham train on 22nd May 1965. The service ended three weeks later. *John Beckett*

Back cover: Producing a smoke effect out of all proportion to its size, No.W36 *Carisbrooke* attempts to blacken the entire Isle of Wight as it pulls away from Ryde St. John's Road station with a Ventnor line train in April 1962. A novice fireman, perhaps? *Derek Penney*

Title Page: Between Midford and Radstock the Somerset & Dorset line followed, as closely as possible, the course of an old plateway built to convey coal from the mines around Radstock to the canal system at Midford. The tramway kept closely to the sides of the valleys and was bedevilled with notoriously tight curves which the engineers building the S&D endeavoured to follow, thus precluding any prospect of fast running. On some stretches however, the curves were so sharp that not even the S&D could follow them! In this shot S&D 2-8-0 No.53806 is depicted near Shoscombe & Single Hill Halt with the Cleethorpes to Exmouth through train on 5th August 1961. *John Beckett*

Introduction

The purpose of this book is to present a representative selection of photographs of branch line steam on the Southern Region taken during the last ten years or so of operation. It is a companion volume to 'Southern Counties Main Line Steam' that was published in 2011. The geographical area covered by the book comprises what are generally regarded as the 'Southern Counties' of England, consequently the 'West Country' counties of Devon and Cornwall have been excluded. I omitted the Somerset & Dorset (S&D) line from the first volume on the basis that for most of the year it had the atmosphere of a branch line and really only came into its own as a 'main line' carrying heavy holiday traffic to the South Coast on just a few Saturdays at the height of the summer season. The S&D is, therefore, included in this book plus, of course, the delightful Isle of Wight system which, in steam days, had an individual character all of its own.

It is sometimes said that the Great Western Railway (GWR) was a system composed of many branch lines but, at least in the author's view, the 'Southern' (Southern Railway) also boasted a large number of fascinating and very historic branches to rival those of the GWR and surely it can be fairly said that on the 'Southern' there was a much greater variety of motive power. Remarkably, one of the very first branch lines to be built in Great Britain is in the area covered by this book, and also one of the last. The Canterbury & Whitstable Railway (C&WR) was incorporated by an Act of Parliament on 10th June 1825 and the line opened for traffic on 3rd May 1830. It remained open for passengers until 1st January 1931 and was closed completely on 28th February 1953. The C&WR may have had a life of well over a hundred years but the nearby line from Stoke Junction to Allhallows-on-Sea, on the Isle of Grain, in complete contrast, was not so lucky managing an operating life of only just over 30 years. The 'Southern' wished to exploit what they thought was the vast potential for a major holiday resort at Allhallows and in 1932 they opened a branch to the 'resort' across the flat and featureless terrain from Stoke Junction, on the Gravesend to Port Victoria line. The line's advocates were soon proved to be hopelessly over-optimistic and their plans to develop a resort to rival Margate came to nothing – the route was closed in December 1961. Besides the two branches mentioned above, another branch line with a particular claim to fame is also featured in this volume. This is the short section from Brockenhurst (Lymington Junction) to Lymington Pier which became the last passenger branch to be worked by steam traction. Diesel-electric multiple units replaced steam from 3rd April 1967 but their use was only an interim measure until electric traction took over three months later. Ironically, the branch is once again largely diesel-worked.

Most of the branches depicted in this book saw occasional infiltration by diesel locomotives and multiple units and, indeed, some were completely dieselised but, in many cases, the introduction of diesel traction failed to stave off closure despite the enhanced service that was often provided. Other lines, however, retained steam on timetabled services right until the end, notable examples being the Hawkhurst branch, the Horsham to Guildford line and the Somerset & Dorset (S&D). Perhaps the best-known system where steam traction survived unchallenged was that on the Isle of Wight, where the physical isolation of the island deterred the introduction of more modern motive power and guaranteed the system's unique atmosphere. Thus, the ancient O2 Class 0-4-4Ts, hauling beautifully maintained trains of vintage carriages, ensured that the island became a place of pilgrimage for 'Southern' steam fans, many of whom flocked across to Ryde to enjoy delightful and relaxing pre-grouping travel that it was no longer possible to experience on the mainland in normal BR service.

The withdrawal of railway passenger services in the 1960s was a contentious issue and sometimes large crowds of people, many of whom had probably not travelled by train for many years, were drawn to their local station to witness the last train. Saturday 2nd May 1964 was a very sad day in Hampshire because that was the day when the final trains ran to three towns in the county, Wimborne, Ringwood and Fordingbridge on the Bournemouth to Brockenhurst and Salisbury lines. In times gone by the Fordingbridge line was once the haunt of graceful T9 Class 4-4-0s on passenger workings and 700 Class 0-6-0s on goods trips, but by the mid-1960s 'Moguls' of both 'Southern' and BR origin were the usual motive power.

On the last day it is recorded that No.76066 worked the 4.50pm Bournemouth West to Salisbury train and 8.30pm return while, most unusually, an un-rebuilt Bulleid Pacific, No.34091 *Weymouth*, was turned out to power the 5.20pm Salisbury to Bournemouth and 7.50pm back, both of which had been specially strengthened to eight coaches to accommodate 'last day' revellers. The former locomotive carried a commemorative headboard and wreath, while on arrival at Fordingbridge the 7.50pm *ex*-Bournemouth was greeted by a large crowd of sightseers. Both trains were festooned with 'streamers' (toilet rolls) which had been kindly provided by BR!

Some of the routes featured in this album are still busy today, but most have long since been erased from the landscape and one is left to ponder whether the orgy of closures in the 1960s was prudent, bearing in mind the development that many towns have experienced since those days when car travel and expansion of the road system seemed to be the only way ahead. Once again I would like to express my appreciation to all the photographers who have trusted me with the precious transparencies: production of this book would not have been possible without their assistance. In addition, John Beckett, Chris Evans, Dave Fakes, John Langford, Graham Mallinson, Terry Phillips and Ian Wright have suggested many corrections and improvements which have greatly enhanced the end product and I am most grateful to these gentlemen. The luggage labels were kindly provided by Les Dench. Design and typesetting by Lucy Frontani and Laura Tristram. I accept responsibility for any errors that have remained undetected.

Michael Welch
Burgess Hill, West Sussex
June 2012

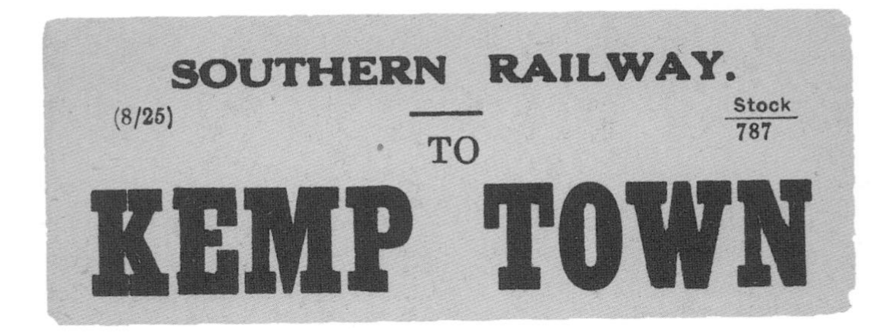

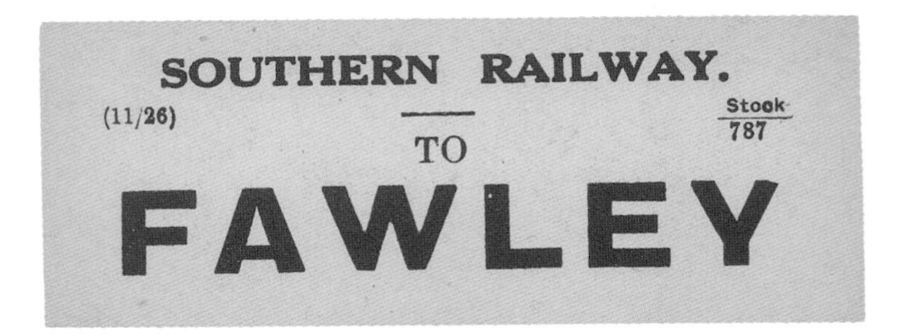

Contents

Strangely, perhaps, the first branch line to feature in the main part of this book has little in common with the others, being constructed solely for boat train traffic to Folkestone Harbour station. The branch did not convey local passenger or goods traffic. The South Eastern Railway (SER) opened the line in 1849 and improvements to the harbour carried out in 1885 enabled regular timetabled sailings to be introduced regardless of the tides. In past times there was a very extensive layout at Folkestone Harbour consisting of a large goods yard and warehouse east of the station while on the western side a bank of carriage sidings occupied a substantial area between the shoreline and Marine Parade. In each case access to the yards could only be gained by running through the station and along the pier for a distance before reversing into the yards – hardly a convenient arrangement, but one made necessary by the awkward and restricted layout of the site. Some hotels on the seafront provided a grandstand view of the carriage sidings with the sea no doubt visible in the background. One wonders if they advertised a 'sea view' in their brochures; surely guests would have felt the hotels were guilty of deception. In BR days the installations at Folkestone Harbour were gradually reduced, goods traffic being withdrawn in August 1968. In this photograph, taken in September 1960, a boat train is seen crossing the viaduct that separated the inner and outer harbours with a former Great Western Railway pannier tank locomotive banking at the rear. The leading engine has just reached the foot of the very steep 1 in 30 incline up to Folkestone Junction, where the train would have reversed and a main-line locomotive taken over for the run up to London. This short branch provided one of the most stirring displays of raw steam power in the south of England. *Colour-Rail.com*

A line through the 'garden of England'. The 11½ miles-long Hawkhurst branch diverged from the main Tonbridge to Dover line east of Paddock Wood station and penetrated deep into rural Kent, an area noted for its hop gardens, apple orchards and numerous oast houses. A number of abortive attempts were made to bring a railway to this part of the High Weald, but eventually in 1892 the SER opened a branch from Paddock Wood to Hope Mill (later Goudhurst) and Hawkhurst was reached in September 1893. In this picture a very dirty South Eastern & Chatham Railway (SECR) C Class 0-6-0 No.31588 is seen leaving Paddock Wood station with the 4.25pm train to Hawkhurst on 10th June 1961, the last day of regular services. The coach immediately behind the locomotive is a Maunsell-designed second class saloon vehicle dating from the early 1930s, which is part of a 'pull-push' set. The train is passing underneath Paddock Wood's impressive elevated signal box which was earmarked for closure once the resignalling plans for the main line came to fruition. Note the brand new electric multiple unit on the right. *John Beckett*

The empty stock of a hop pickers' special bound for Hawkhurst passes through the hop gardens between Horsmonden and Goudhurst on 11th September 1960. Motive power is provided by C Class No.31588; this is the engine seen in the previous shot so presumably it was a 'regular' on the Hawkhurst line. A lovely photograph that beautifully encapsulates the character of the branch. *John Langford*

A poster, photographed on Goudhurst station on 10th June 1961, advises passengers of the imminent closure of the Hawkhurst branch and whom to contact regarding the alternative public transport available. *Stuart Ackley collection*

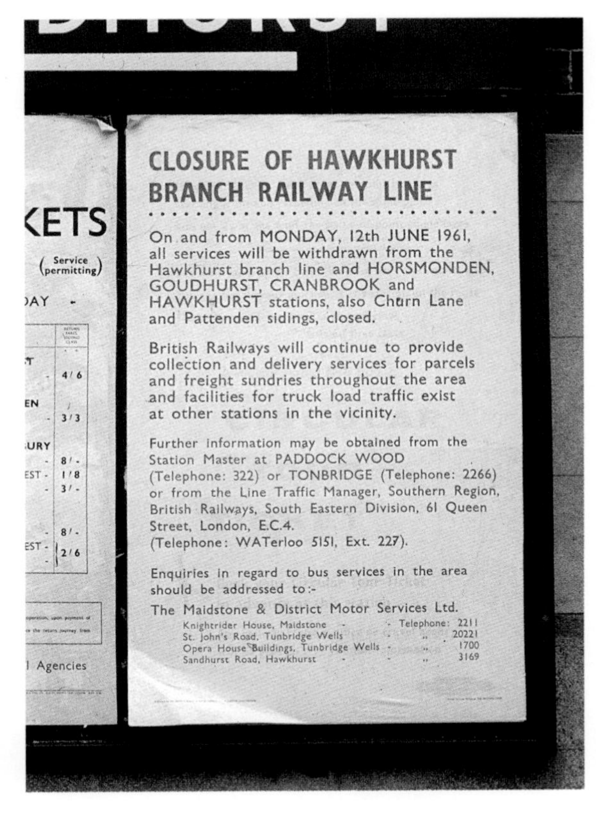

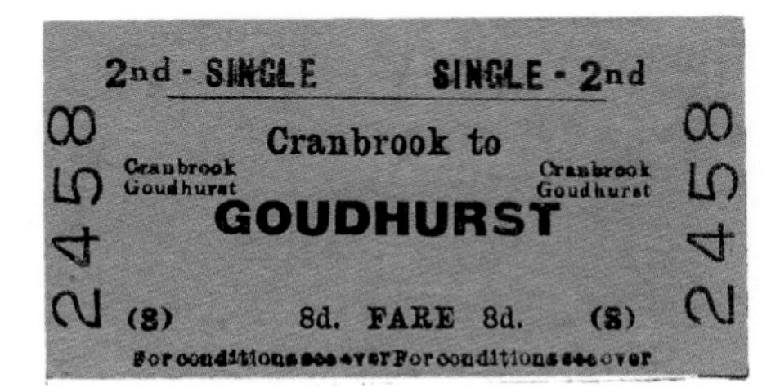

Substantial wooden level crossing gates, a cream-and-green-painted signal box and a large running-in board which left passengers in no doubt about the identity of the station. This was the scene at Goudhurst, looking southwards towards Hawkhurst on a summer's day just prior to closure. Many branch lines suffered from the age-old problem of having stations some distance from the settlements they were supposed to serve and the Hawkhurst branch was no exception, the village of Goudhurst being a mile away and 300ft higher than the station. The gentleman standing in the doorway is Mr Edwin Wilmshurst, the well-known railway and shipping enthusiast. *Gerald Daniels*

31580

Cranbrook station in the wintertime. The platform and points have been cleared but everything else is buried under a few inches of snow. The stationmaster's house here was almost identical to that at Goudhurst, being a tall, slender three-storey building constructed of brick. This must have been a really quiet spot but probably not much fun for any children living there who could not simply 'pop next door' to play with friends. Passenger facilities at Cranbrook appear to have been rather basic and provided by an unpretentious single-storey building of corrugated iron, but at least there was a reasonable canopy which protected travellers from the rain and provided some shade on a hot summer day. The building just beyond the house is the small signal box. *Gerald Daniels*

Opposite Cranbrook was another station which was some way from the place it purported to serve, in this case being about two miles distant, and its isolation is clearly apparent from this picture, the premises being surrounded by open countryside. The only habitation in view, apart from the station house, is the caravans parked in the field in the background. The immediate impression one gets from this picture is of a busy scene showing a C Class locomotive shunting a branch goods working but, in reality, this photograph was taken after the closure (note the blank running-in board) and shows a train merely collecting wagons prior to track lifting. Perhaps, apart from demolition trains, this was the *very* last working. This shot was taken on 20th June 1961. *Gerald Daniels*

The station facilities provided for passengers at Hawkhurst may not have been the most lavish but other infrastructure was much more substantial. Remarkable though it may seem there was an engine shed at Hawkhurst which is clearly visible in the middle of the picture beyond the bracket signal. It was a two-road structure and is understood to have been taken out of use in the early 1930s. Note also the solidly constructed water tank and brightly painted signal box, plus part of the goods shed wall which is just visible on the extreme right of the photograph. Like other stations on the line, Hawkhurst was a considerable distance from the town it was built to serve, the town centre being situated two miles distant and at a higher altitude than the station, so those without transport were faced with a mainly uphill walk to the town. The passenger service towards the end consisted of about half a dozen trains on weekdays and there was some goods traffic on the line, principally coal and flowers, but the traffic with the highest profile was probably the hop pickers' trains that ran from London during the season. The mechanisation of hop picking, growing private car ownership and poor connections at Paddock Wood, all combined to make operations on the branch totally uneconomic and the line was closed completely from 12th June 1961. *Stuart Ackley collection*

Hawkhurst station on (what appears to be) a warm summer's day with puffy clouds scudding across the horizon; set No.732 sits in the platform before forming the next train back to Paddock Wood. Everything on the station looks really spic and span and it is sad to reflect that the line was facing oblivion. There was a very short shunting neck here and, consequently, 4-4-0 and 0-6-0 tender engines were the largest locomotives permitted on the branch. The station was laid out as a through station because, apparently, there were plans at one time to extend the line beyond Hawkhurst – obviously there was no shortage of unrestrained optimism – but these never materialised. Note the very basic station buildings provided here, but at least the premises are enhanced by a splendid Southern Railway vintage running-in board supported on iron posts and an elegant 'barley sugar' oil lamp. The train occupying the platform is a steam-worked 'pull-push' set with the driving cab prominent, the locomotive being out of view at the other end of the train.
Stuart Ackley collection

The early success of Allhallows-on-Sea as a resort for day trippers prompted the Southern Railway to provide new down platforms and nameboards at Cliffe and Sharnal Street stations plus a crossing loop at Cliffe. All of the new equipment was constructed at the Exmouth Junction concrete works. Here is the 1934-built down platform at Cliffe and the SER signalbox (re-opened in 1934), both looking sadly neglected in this view which was taken on 14th October 1961 in the last days of passenger service on the branch. Like so many country stations, most of the village was more than a mile away and local people looked more to the Medway towns than to Gravesend. Connections to and from London were tolerably good however, some 70 minutes being the average journey time. The station master at Cliffe had responsibility for the entire Hundred of Hoo branch, which had considerable goods traffic for the Royal Navy at Chattenden and industries at Kingsnorth, even before the building of the major oil refinery at Grain in the early 1950s. *John Langford*

The railway line to the Isle of Grain was originally established on 11th September 1882 when the South Eastern Railway opened its eleven miles-long branch from Gravesend (Hoo Junction) to Port Victoria. The SER had grandiose plans for Port Victoria and planned to develop the port in competition with the rival London, Chatham & Dover Railway (LCDR) but the two companies amalgamated in 1899 thus making a competing service pointless and, furthermore, the pier was declared unsafe in about 1916. In its heyday boat trains ran from London to Port Victoria to connect with sailings to Belgium and European heads of state once walked along its platforms. Passenger traffic on the Port Victoria branch subsequently declined and the station closed on 11th June 1951. A brand new station was opened at Grain on 3rd September 1951 to serve a new oil refinery, the station being located immediately east of Grain Crossing Halt. The line from Grain to Gravesend traversed a thinly populated landscape, the passenger service eventually succumbing on 4th December 1961. This photograph, taken at Grain in the early 1960s, shows the oil refinery in the distance but the most interesting feature is the design of the very distinctive signal box which presumably dated from the early 1950s, when the new station was opened. *Gerald Daniels*

The branch to Allhallows – an unfulfilled dream. On 14th May 1932 the Southern Railway opened a new line which ran 1¾ miles from Stoke Junction, on the Gravesend to Port Victoria line, to the tiny village of Allhallows. The 'Southern', who worked in conjunction with a land developer, had high hopes of creating a major seaside resort alongside the Thames estuary to rival places like Margate and Broadstairs, and a medium-sized terminal station was constructed in the standard style of the period. The branch was doubled shortly after opening and through trains operated from London for a while and there was also a reasonably heavy traffic in day-trippers on Sundays and bank holidays. Despite their best efforts the Southern Railway's idea never caught the public's imagination and windswept Allhallows remained a sleepy village, its population increasing only marginally between 1930 and 1960. A few holiday caravans are visible in the background of this shot of smartly turned-out SECR H Class 0-4-4T No.31512 which was working a Railway Enthusiasts Club rail tour on 24th September 1960. The long platform canopy, which bears testament to the railway's ambitious plans, will be noted. The branch was closed completely from 4th December 1961, the same day that the trains to Grain were withdrawn, from which date the Allhallows branch disappeared from the railway map, its principal claim to fame being its extremely short existence. *John Langford*

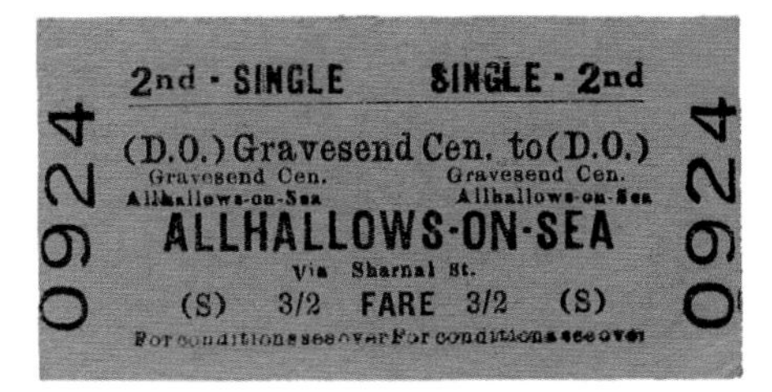

The line between Robertsbridge and Headcorn via Tenterden was originally opened as the Rother Valley Railway and was part of Colonel Stephens' light railway empire. Light railways were usually cheaply constructed, civil engineering works being kept to a minimum, and they were often laid in rural areas where construction of an ordinary standard-gauge line could not be justified. The Rother Valley Railway opened to passengers from Robertsbridge to Rolvenden on 2nd April 1900 and soon gained a reputation as an eccentric, rather ramshackle concern run on a shoestring. In 1904 it changed its name to the Kent & East Sussex Railway. Despite its eccentricity the railway managed to build an extension to Headcorn, on the SECR London to Folkestone main line, this opening on 15th May 1905. The railway owned a motley collection of steam locomotives from a variety of sources and, in the 1920s/30s, operated petrol-driven twin railcars. The line escaped the Grouping in 1923 but fierce competition from bus services started at about this time eroding its traffic, and the section north of Tenterden began to lose money. Nationalised in 1948, the line became a troublesome appendage of the Southern Region who closed the entire route to passengers in early 1954, leaving only the section south of Tenterden open for goods workings. Apart from a short stub at Robertsbridge, which lasted some years longer to serve a flour mill, the remainder was closed in June 1961. Here, a Locomotive Club of Great Britain rail tour with a London, Brighton & South Coast Railway (LBSCR) 'Terrier' in charge (assisted by another 'Terrier' at the other end of the train) waits to leave the former Tenterden Town station with the final train under BR auspices, on 11th June 1961. *Gerald Daniels*

The KESR may have been run on a shoestring, but when it came to cast iron trespass notices no expense seems to have been spared and the examples found on the line seemed to have been well up to standard. This one, photographed near Bodiam on 11th June 1961, was still in good condition after nearly 50 years' exposure to the wind and rain. *John Beckett*

The KESR ran through some quiet countryside, passing hop gardens and the impressive Bodiam castle and, despite the demise of the northern stretch beyond Tenterden, its attractions were not lost on rail tour operators. These trains were usually quite heavy by KESR standards and were normally powered by two LBSCR 'Terriers', one at each end of the train. In this picture No.32636 is depicted at the rear of a Branch Line Society rail tour which is waiting to leave Northiam *en route* for Tenterden on 12th April 1958. This diminutive locomotive was built in 1872 and sold out of service to the Newhaven Harbour Company in 1898. It returned to the Southern Railway in 1925 and survived to become the oldest working locomotive in the BR fleet. Upon withdrawal it was purchased for preservation by the Bluebell Railway but it is not operational at the time of writing. *Derek Penney*

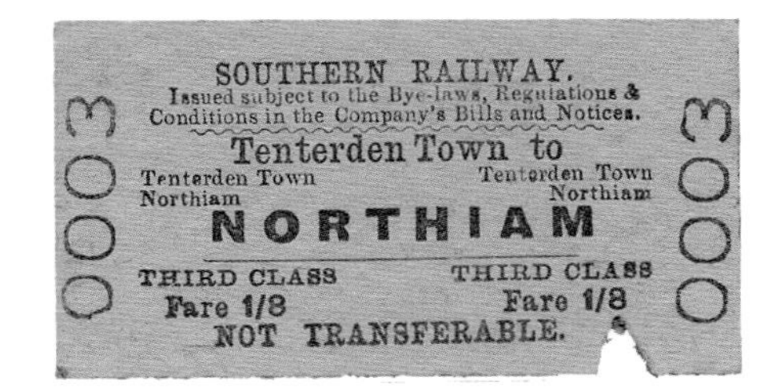
0003

SOUTHERN RAILWAY.
Issued subject to the Bye-laws, Regulations & Conditions in the Company's Bills and Notices.
Tenterden Town to

Tenterden Town
Northiam

Tenterden Town
Northiam

NORTHIAM

THIRD CLASS
Fare 1/8

THIRD CLASS
Fare 1/8

NOT TRANSFERABLE.

0003

The 10 miles-long line from Paddock Wood to Maidstone West was approved in 1843 and opened on 25th September 1844. Later an extension to Strood was constructed, following an Act of Parliament passed in 1853, and this section opened on 18th June 1856. Apart from an initial 2 miles-long section at the southern end of the route the line parallels the river Medway and, though certainly not spectacular, the Paddock Wood to Maidstone stretch offers some very pleasant river scenery. The first station of any importance after leaving Paddock Wood is Yalding, and in this illustration former SECR H Class 0-4-4T No.31305 is seen passing over a level crossing and entering the station with a Sevenoaks to Maidstone West train on 20th May 1961. This may seem to the casual observer to be a somewhat circuitous route, but at the time of this photograph both Sevenoaks and Maidstone West were at the limit of the suburban electrified area and it was, therefore, logical to run a steam-operated service between them. This ceased when electric working was introduced from 12th June 1961. Note that there is a northbound diesel-hauled goods train standing on the up line: presumably the Yalding signalman had decided to allow the passenger train to overtake. *John Beckett*

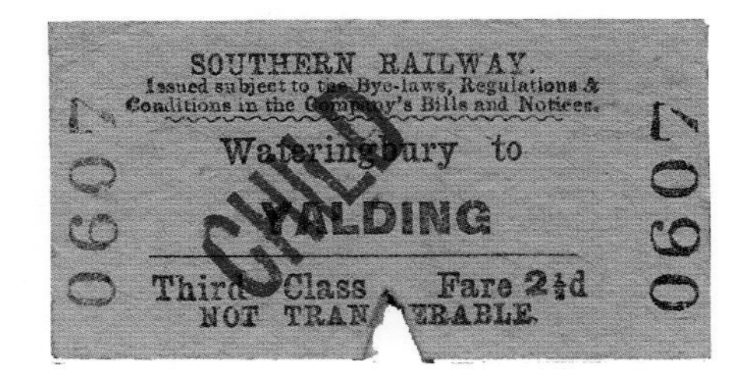

0607 SOUTHERN RAILWAY. 0607
Issued subject to the Bye-laws, Regulations & Conditions in the Company's Bills and Notices.
Wateringbury to
YALDING
CHILD
Third Class Fare 2½d
NOT TRANSFERABLE.

The Paddock Wood to Maidstone line, as previously mentioned, offers some very pleasant riverside scenery and in this picture SECR C Class 0-6-0 No.31244 is seen getting into its stride after leaving Wateringbury with a Maidstone West to Sevenoaks working, also on 20th May 1961. The river Medway is visible on the right of the shot. No.31244 was built at Ashford works in April 1902 and survived in service until October 1961. The train is made up of a BR Standard 3-set plus a Maunsell carriage which is, judging by the low height corridor sidelights, an example of one of his earliest designs, probably dating from around 1927. *John Beckett*

The 5.40pm Maidstone West to London Bridge return hop pickers' special, headed by SECR D1 Class 4-4-0 No.31487 hauling seven coaches, is depicted at Wateringbury on Sunday 11th September 1960. This train would have called at all stations to Tonbridge, then Sevenoaks, Orpington and New Cross *en route* to London Bridge. The train's reporting number is prominently displayed on the smokebox door, completely obscuring the engine's number plate. Note that although conductor rails have been laid in preparation for electrification, old-fashioned semaphore signalling remains in use. The SR had decided not to install colour light signalling on newly electrified routes where traffic densities were low and several routes in Kent remained semaphore signalled for many years after electrification.
John Langford

($\frac{5}{27}$) SOUTHERN RAILWAY. ($\frac{\text{Stock}}{\text{787 P}}$)

WATERINGBURY

7 | 8 | 9 | 10 | 11 | 12

4509

BRITISH RAILWAYS (S)
This ticket is issued subject to the Bye-laws, Regulations and Conditions contained in the Publications and Notices of and applicable to the Railway Executive.

PLATFORM TICKET 1d.
Available ONE HOUR on DAY of ISSUE ONLY.
Not valid in Trains. Not Transferable
WATERINGBURY
TO BE GIVEN UP WHEN LEAVING PLATFORM

1 | 2 | 3 | 4 | 5 | 6

4509

WAY OUT
LADIES ROOM
GENTLEMEN
WATERINGBURY

In this photograph, taken at Maidstone West station on a sunny day in 1961, SECR H Class 0-4-4T No.31512 sits in a bay platform with, what is presumably, a train to Tonbridge. This is a rather confusing shot because the locomotive is displaying a white headcode disc, indicating a train to Tonbridge, plus a tail lamp! If it had left the station showing these contradictory indications in gross violation of the regulations, one wonders how far the train would have got before being brought to a halt by an irate signalman waving his rule book! Maidstone West was no doubt an interesting location for observers at this time, with electric multiple units coming and going on trains to Strood, while steam traction still held sway on local workings to Paddock Wood or Tonbridge and beyond. Goods trains were doubtless monopolised by C and Q1 class steam locomotives interspersed with BRCW Type 3 Bo-Bo diesel locomotives which became universally known as 'Cromptons'. *Gerald Daniels*

The early 1960s saw vast changes to the railway system in Kent as steam traction was quickly eliminated in favour of electric traction. Those lines that survived benefited from much improved services, but one type of train that had no place in the new order was the traditional hop pickers' special. Changing lifestyles and, no doubt, increasing prosperity meant that the autumn of 1960 was the last for these trains, and in this illustration SECR D1 Class 4-4-0 No.31487 is seen at Maidstone West before taking the 5.40pm hop pickers' special back to London Bridge via Tonbridge – perhaps one of the last ever workings? This train is also depicted elsewhere in this book, leaving Wateringbury, displaying its reporting number and route discs, these having been put in position at the last minute just before the train left Maidstone. The photographer recalls that earlier in the day E1 Class No.31067 had powered the 8.28am London Bridge to Maidstone West via Tonbridge, connections being made at Paddock Wood with a special train to Hawkhurst with C Class 0-6-0 No.31588 in charge. It appears that local people resented the visits of working class Londoners and some publicans set up trestle tables at the rear of their premises so that the regular clientele was not obliged to mingle with the hop picking fraternity. *John Langford*

Opposite Wayside stations do not come much finer than Wateringbury which is located in a peaceful setting beside the river Medway. The station opened in 1844, but there are doubts that the station building depicted here was built at that time because all the other SER stations built in the 1840s are Classical or Italianate rather than the Tudor style seen here. It is more likely to have been constructed in about 1855, a date that coincides with similar types by William Tress and the almost identical design of the nearby Aylesford station. The original building was extended with various additions between 1886-99. Wateringbury is a red brick, two-storey building with stone quoins and tiled roofs. Note the attractive gables and decorative tall chimneys. What a gem! *Gerald Daniels*

Parliamentary authority to build a branch from Dunton Green, on the London to Tonbridge main line, to Westerham was first obtained by the SER in the early 1860s but it failed to act upon them and nothing happened until local interests secured the incorporation of the Westerham Valley Railway Company in 1876. In 1879 the SER agreed to operate the branch which opened to traffic on 7th July 1881. The 4¾ miles-long line at first had only one intermediate station, at Brasted, but in 1907 the SECR opened Chevening Halt which was located around 1½ miles from the main line junction. It might be supposed that a branch line located so close to the capital would have an assured future but, unfortunately, Westerham was only three or so miles from Oxted, which offered a good service of through trains to both London Bridge and Victoria stations, and many Westerham commuters were doubtless tempted to drive to Oxted and catch a train from there. In 1955 declining patronage along the line resulted in the withdrawal of all off-peak services on Mondays to Fridays, but at the weekends a regular service was still provided throughout the day. Perhaps Westerham's location eventually proved to be its downfall and all services were withdrawn from 30th October 1961. In this picture part of Dunton Green station is depicted on the 29th October with a prominent sign indicating the platform from where Westerham branch trains departed. Note the gas lighting. *Stuart Ackley collection*

6337
SOUTHERN RAILWAY.
This ticket is issued subject to the Company's Bye-laws, Regulations and Conditions in their Time Tables, Notices and Book of Regulations.
Available on DAY of issue ONLY.
Westerham to
Westerham Dunton Green
Westerham Dunton Green
DUNTON GREEN
THIRD CLASS Fare 7½d.
THIRD CLASS Fare 7½d.
6337

Chevening Halt on 14th October 1961 with SECR H Class 0-4-4T No.31530 propelling out of the station with the 4.23pm Westerham to Dunton Green train. *John Beckett*

Somebody has chalked 'The Westerham Flyer Once Called Here' on this redundant BR notice board at Chevening Halt, so it could be assumed that the axing of the service did not exactly meet with the universal approval of the local population. Clearly, insufficient shoppers were tempted by BR's four shilling and nine pence shopping ticket to town. Note the wide open spaces around the station which stretch as far as the eye can see.
Stuart Ackley collection

The only intermediate station on the Westerham branch provided when the line was originally built was at Brasted, where a modest single platform station was constructed. There was no loop at Brasted and trains in both directions used the same platform. The station building, like so many SER stations, had wooden cladding painted in the traditional green and cream colours, but by the early 1960s, when this photograph was taken, the colours had faded considerably. Note the 'barley sugar' gas lamp standard which considerably enhances the scene. The lamp is illuminated, but perhaps this is explained by the fact that the station had become an unstaffed halt and the lamp had to be switched on by the train crew, sometimes well before it was actually needed. *Gerald Daniels*

A Dunton Green to Westerham train pauses at Brasted on 17th August 1961 with SECR H Class 0-4-4T No.31518 in charge. At least two passengers have just alighted and can just be discerned behind the fence. For some years passenger accommodation on this line was provided by two carriages originally built in 1905/06 as rail motor vehicles for the SECR. In the late 1950s the SR was becoming increasingly concerned about the crash worthiness of its fleet of vintage coaches and when the British Transport Commission issued a directive in 1959 stating that all passenger coaches more than 30 years old must be withdrawn this brought matters to a head. The old rail motor stock was replaced in 1960 by 'pull-push' sets which had been formed from surplus, but much more modern, Maunsell stock which is forming the train seen here. *Les Dench*

Photographed towards the end of the station platform, No.31518 propels a train to Dunton Green out of Westerham station, the large running-in board leaving passengers in no doubt regarding the identity of the station. The station's 13-lever signal box is in the middle of the shot. In the early days of the line a locomotive stabled overnight at Westerham, for which a small shed was provided. It is thought that the building survived until about 1925. This view shows another example of a 'pull-push' working displaying a headcode and a tail lamp simultaneously. *Gerald Daniels*

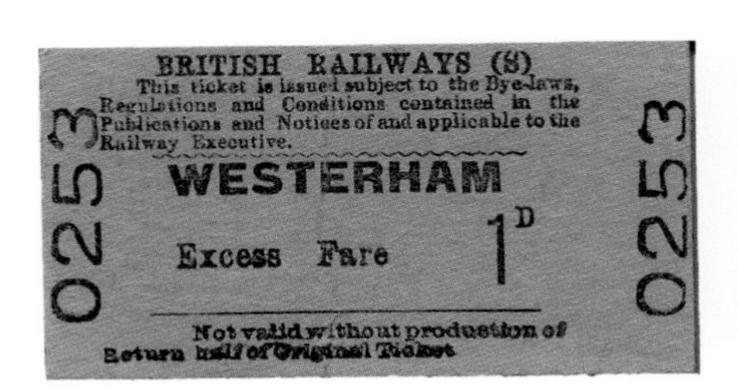

This vintage shunt signal survived at Westerham until the end of the branch. It was photographed on 28th October 1961, the last day of traffic. One wonders when the post was last painted! *John Beckett*

What may well have been the busiest day in its history was also the last for this branch. The 28th October 1961 was a brilliantly sunny day, the ideal weather conditions no doubt encouraging families to go out for a last run over the line – perhaps for some it was also their first! No.31518 operated the usual two-coach passenger service until the early afternoon when D1 Class 4-4-0 No.31739 brought down a seven-coach set from London. The remaining services were worked by No.31739 assisted by Bulleid Q1 Class 0-6-0 No.33029 from Tonbridge shed. These locomotives worked alternate round trips with this set until the final special, the 8.30pm from Westerham, which was handled by the Q1 locomotive. Two engines were needed owing to the limited run-round facilities at Dunton Green. It is, perhaps, surprising that a line so close to London succumbed to closure but much of the trackbed was later used for a motorway scheme. No.31739 poses at Westerham after arrival with the 2.50pm train from Dunton Green. *Colour-Rail.com*

Fierce gradients, glorious Sussex Wealden scenery and impressive station buildings.....there is no doubt that the Eastbourne to Tunbridge Wells line is one of the most appealing featured in this album. The Polegate to Eridge (Redgate Mill Junction) section was universally known as the 'Cuckoo Line', the route taking its name from the Cuckoo Fair held annually at Heathfield. The line was opened in three sections, the first between Polegate and Hailsham carrying its first passengers on 14th May 1849. There was a very long wait until the second stretch of line opened to Heathfield on 3rd April 1880, followed soon afterwards by the final part of the line to Eridge which opened on 1st September. The long gap was partly a result of problems in the banking world which caused funds for railway building to evaporate and endless wrangling between the LBSCR and the SER. Remarkably, four stations in succession have names beginning with the letter 'H', the second of which is the smallest station on the line, Hellingly. The station here served only a tiny village and was noteworthy as the only one on the line without a passing loop. In many ways Hellingly station was the most interesting due to the presence of the East Sussex Lunatic Asylum, about a mile to the east, which opened in 1905. A private siding, which was electrified at 500volts dc on the overhead principle, ran from the station conveying patients, staff and visitors. There was even some coal traffic and all trains were worked by four-wheeled steeple-cab locomotives. This little system closed to passengers in 1931 but remained open for goods until 1959. The exterior of Hellingly station is seen here on 12th June 1965. This was built in mock Tudor style with wooden beams and flower patterns, but all of this decoration was hidden by hanging tiles in 1890 in order to protect the building from the elements. *Stuart Ackley collection*

Horam station is the setting for this picture of Bulleid 'Battle of Britain' Pacific No.34066 *Spitfire* passing with a rail tour on a rather gloomy 22nd March 1964. This train's itinerary was really ingenious and managed to cover a large number of Sussex branch lines, including the Guildford to Horsham branch, Steyning line and the Three Bridges to Tunbridge Wells section. After leaving Tunbridge Wells the train ran down the 'Cuckoo Line' and the participants were later treated to a trip along the Kemp Town branch before returning to London via Uckfield. Horam station was known as 'Waldron and Horeham Road' at one time, the abbreviation to 'Horam' being adopted in the mid 1950s. Incredibly, in times gone by there were two signal boxes at Horam but these were replaced by an 18-lever frame on the up platform in 1935. Milk traffic was important here and even justified the provision of a siding into the Express Dairy Company's premises, this being laid in 1935 during the signalling changes. *Ken Wightman/ David Clark collection*

Unfortunately, despite the line's unquestionable attractions, colour pictures of ordinary steam trains on the 'Cuckoo Line' are hard to find, perhaps because of the early dieselisation of many week-end services. In this photograph another rail tour is depicted, this time the Locomotive Club of Great Britain's (LCGB) 'Sussex Coast Limited' which ran on 24th June 1962. This special also boasted a fascinating itinerary including the Guildford to Horsham line plus the Midhurst branch which was still open for goods traffic at that time. The preserved London & South Western Railway T9 Class 4-4-0 No.120, then recently restored to its pre-grouping livery, was booked to haul the train from Haywards Heath to Eastbourne and, after turning at Eastbourne shed, from there to East Grinstead via Heathfield. The operating authorities were taking no chances, however, and M7 Class 0-4-4T No.30055 was provided to pilot the T9 over the heaviest 'Cuckoo Line' grades from Eastbourne as far as Rotherfield. Here this quite unusual combination is seen entering Heathfield. *Alan Chandler*

Closure of the 'Cuckoo Line' was proposed in the Beeching Report and, after the usual legal formalities, partial closure was approved by the Minister of Transport and subsequently the SR announced that the last passenger trains would run on 13th June 1965, the line officially closing from the following day. The section from Polegate to Hailsham was reprieved, while goods trains continued to run as far as Heathfield, but the line north of Heathfield was axed completely. The Guildford to Horsham line was also scheduled for closure from 14th June, so this gave the LCGB a golden opportunity to sponsor a tour covering both routes prior to closure with other threatened lines included. The train was titled 'The Wealdsman' and in this view a pair of Maunsell 'Moguls', Nos.31803 and 31411, are seen leaving Heathfield; in the foreground enthusiasts have lined up to take a farewell photograph. The station here, the busiest on the line, had a large goods yard but its most notable claim to fame concerns the discovery of natural gas when a water borehole was being deepened in 1896. The station's lighting was converted to burn the gas, but plans by a local company to exploit the find for commercial purposes came to nought. *John Beckett*

LCGB
THE
SUSSEX COAST LIMITED
RAIL TOUR
LCGB
No 120
281285

Rotherfield and Mark Cross station on 4th June 1965 with an unidentified BR Standard Class 4MT 2-6-4T pausing with an Eastbourne train. Like all of the line's stations, Rotherfield was really impressive and had a commodious stationmaster's house and quite generous canopies on both platforms. Unfortunately, there were no immediate centres of population: both Rotherfield and Mark Cross villages were some distance away and the station was located in a tranquil location surrounded by woodland and unspoilt Wealden countryside. Note the electric lighting – clearly Rotherfield station was not blessed with a natural gas supply! *Colour-Rail*

Opposite Here the LCGB's 'Sussex Coast Limited' rail tour, which is seen in a previous picture entering Heathfield, poses at the north end of Rotherfield station with LSWR preserved T9 Class No.120 in charge on 24th June 1962. The veteran T9 had the assistance of M7 Class No.30055 as far as Rotherfield, but this had obviously been detached because its services were no longer required, the rest of the run being within the T9's capabilities. Note the unfortunate gentleman in the wheelchair looking on from the down platform. *John Langford*

Hauling a rake of four Maunsell coaches, BR Standard 2-6-4T No.80085 passes Birchden Junction with a Tunbridge Wells West to Eastbourne train on 2nd June 1962. This is the spot where the lines from Oxted and Tunbridge Wells converged just north of Eridge station; the Oxted line can be clearly seen behind the fourth coach of the train. No.80085 spent some years on the London Midland Region at Bletchley shed before moving to the SR as part of an exchange for LMSR-designed Fairburn tank locomotives. It was built at Brighton works, emerging in May 1954, and lasted in service until the end of steam on the 'Southern' in July 1967. The large house just visible between the trees on the left of the picture is Glen Andred, an early work of the architect Norman Shaw. *John Beckett*

Groombridge Junction, where the lines from Eridge and Ashurst converged, was a distinctive location but probably one that only attracted photographers during the summer months – its position in a deep, tree-lined cutting doubtless ensured that the sun did not penetrate much during the winter. Two strategically placed bridges gave bystanders an excellent view of passing trains. There were certainly no problems with the sun when this picture of BR Standard Class 4MT 2-6-4T No.80016 hauling a northbound train was taken in June 1963. Note the very severe speed restriction across the junction. Hopefully the local permanent way gang were proud of their concrete hut, positioned on the site of the former Grove Junction signal box, which appears to be brand new. *Martin Smith*

A rather grimy Maunsell 'Mogul' No.31868, of Redhill shed, is depicted near Groombridge with (what appears to be) an Eastbourne to Tunbridge Wells West train in June 1963. The locomotive is 'blowing off' so it is safe to assume that it was not being unduly taxed by its featherweight two-coach load! By the time of this picture many Maunsell four-coach sets had been split to form two separate sets and trains formed of only two coaches were not uncommon. *Martin Smith*

Pictured against a backdrop of lush water meadows, woodland and a lovely sky with puffy clouds, an unidentified BR Standard Class 4MT 2-6-4T, apparently hauling a train from Eastbourne, accelerates past the photographer. This shot was taken between Groombridge and Tunbridge Wells West on 14th October 1961. The driver clearly opened the regulator at just the right time! Spa Valley Railway steam trains can be photographed today at this attractive location. *John Beckett*

The station name on the totem immediately identifies the location of this picture. The train is the 3.08pm from Three Bridges to East Grinstead with nicely cleaned M7 Class 0-4-4T No.30055 in charge. This locomotive was built at Nine Elms and out-shopped in December 1905; it survived in traffic until September 1963. This part of Three Bridges station had the benefit of an overall roof and, unlike the rest of the station, was largely unaffected by the quadrupling of the Brighton Line that occurred before the First World War.
John Beckett

7 | 8 | 9 | 10 | 11 | 12
8326
BRITISH RAILWAYS (S)
THREE BRIDGES
(S.1) PLATFORM TICKET 1d.
Available ONE HOUR on Day of Issue only
NOT VALID IN TRAINS. NOT TRANSFERABLE
To be given up when leaving Platform
FOR CONDITIONS SEE BACK
8326
1 | 2 | 3 | 4 | 5 | 6

SOUTHERN RAILWAY.
(2/46) 12M
Stock 787
TO
THREE BRIDGES

The branch line from Three Bridges, on the London to Brighton Line, to Tunbridge Wells was opened in two separate stages, the first section from Three Bridges to East Grinstead being opened for business on 9th July 1855. The East Grinstead, Groombridge & Tunbridge Wells Railway opened the section onwards to the Kentish spa town on 1st October 1866 but it should be noted that this local concern was immediately absorbed by the LBSCR. The first station reached by trains travelling eastwards from Three Bridges was Rowfant, where a particularly attractive and pleasant station was built for Curtis Miranda Lampson, a local landowner who had sacrificed a strip of his land to enable the railway to be built. Rowfant station was a real gem, primarily provided for this gentleman, and one of the special features of the decorative main building was the alcove for use by his coachman during wet weather. In this illustration SECR H Class 0-4-4T No.31263 is seen propelling a Three Bridges-bound train out of the station on 19th August 1962 as the signalman looks on. *Colour-Rail.com*

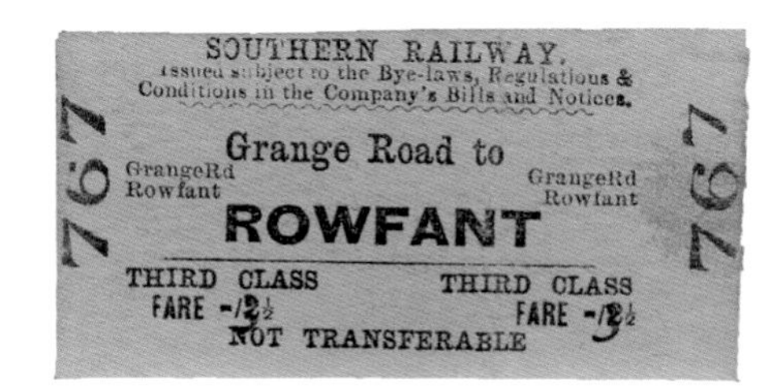

Another shot at Rowfant, this time looking in the other direction towards East Grinstead. This picture shows Maunsell Q Class 0-6-0 No.30547 coming off the single line and entering the westbound platform with a lengthy goods train on 4th April 1963. Twenty of these engines were built in 1938/39 to replace older classes on branch line and secondary duties and the class was one of the last designs of traditional 0-6-0 tender locomotives to be constructed in Great Britain. This particular example was out-shopped from Eastleigh in July 1939 and survived in traffic until January 1964, so 1963 was its last full year in service. *Martin Smith*

A truly evocative branch line scene. There were only two intermediate stations between Three Bridges and East Grinstead, Rowfant and Grange Road, and the last named is depicted in this shot which epitomises the unhurried and relaxed atmosphere which could still be experienced on many branch lines in the early 1960s. It was not possible to cross trains here so the signalman could not have been very busy. Here, former SECR H Class 0-4-4T No.31551 'blows off' in the platform as it awaits the 'right away' with an East Grinstead train on 9th June 1963. This locomotive lasted in service until January 1964 when it was withdrawn, together with sister engines Nos. 31263 and 31518, thus rendering the class extinct on BR. No.31263 was destined to survive into preservation, however, and at the time of writing is nearing the end of a lengthy overhaul at the Bluebell Railway. It is likely to have re-entered traffic by the time this book is published. *Michael Chown*

A section of line between East Grinstead and Tunbridge Wells West ran through the valley of the infant river Medway, the course of which can be seen in this portrait of BR Standard Class 4MT 2-6-4T No.80149 heading a Victoria to Tunbridge Wells train. This picture was taken east of Withyham on 2nd June 1962. The scenery on the line east of East Grinstead is much more open and the character of the trains is also different – certainly, six-coach trains of Bulleid carriages were never seen forming ordinary passenger workings between Three Bridges and East Grinstead! *John Beckett*

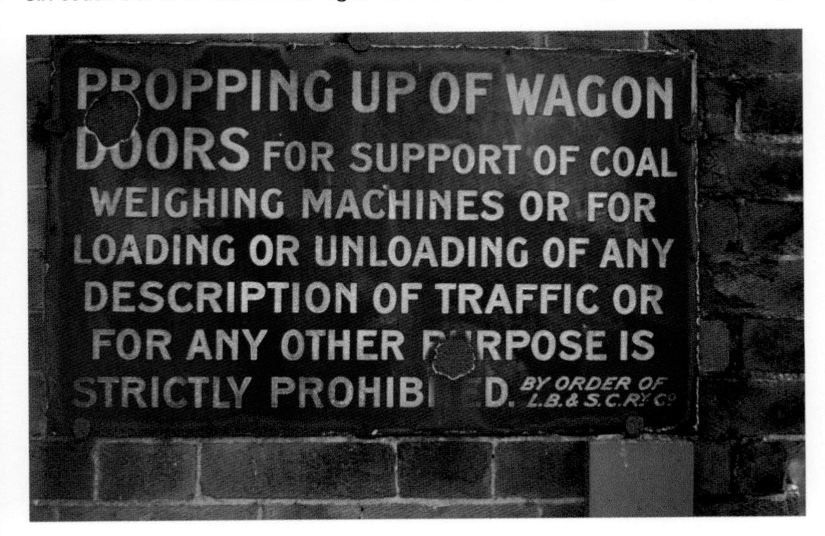

An amazing survivor! This LBSCR warning notice was still displayed in the goods yard at Tunbridge Wells West when this picture was taken on 22nd July 1961. One wonders how it escaped the attention of 'souvenir hunters' for so long. *John Beckett*

Fifteen W Class 2-6-4Ts were constructed to Maunsell's design, five being built at Eastleigh in 1932 while the remainder were constructed at Ashford in 1935/36. They incorporated the side tanks and other parts of the ill-fated 'River' Class locomotives and had three cylinders, components being interchangeable with the N1 and U1 Classes. These engines were confined to goods workings throughout their lives, mostly transfer trips across London, and in the early 1960s all members of the class were based at London area sheds, principally Hither Green and Norwood Junction. In late 1962, however, following increasing dieselisation of cross-London trip working, a batch of these locomotives was sent westwards to Exmouth Junction shed where they replaced the Maunsell Z Class 0-8-0Ts on banking duties between Exeter St. David's and Central stations. They were not successful on this work however, due to lack of adhesion compared to the Z Class engines, and the class simply faded away, many being withdrawn in 1963 while the last example was condemned in August 1964. In this picture a nicely cleaned No.31925 is seen at Hurst Green Junction with a coal train in June 1963; this locomotive stayed in the London area until the end. *Martin Smith*

The W Class engines may have looked reasonably well proportioned when viewed from the front but when seen from the rear......well, not even their best friends would call them handsome. In this portrait No.31919 is also seen at Hurst Green Junction, but this time the train is an up Fyffes banana working from Lingfield. Fyffes had a ripening shed there and the photographer comments that this was a regular Saturday working at the time. This shot was taken on 8th June 1963 and this locomotive was another member of the class that never ventured westwards. It was taken out of traffic at Norwood Junction shed five months after this photograph was taken. *Michael Chown*

The author has compiled around thirty books, the first of which appeared in 1980, but this is the first decent colour picture he has had submitted of a steam train about to plunge into a smoke-filled tunnel. Why were so few pictures of this type taken? The location is the south end of Oxted tunnel and this masterpiece shows an unidentified Maunsell N Class 2-6-0 working a Tunbridge Wells West to London Bridge train on 1st June 1963. The photographer had been intending to take a frontal view, but decided to opt for this shot due to the large amount of smoke from the preceding banana train hauled by a W Class 2-6-4T. What a brilliant decision! *Michael Chown*

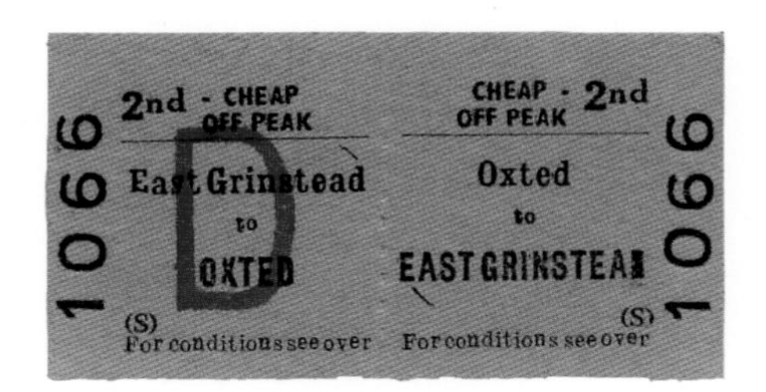

Super power on the Oxted Line! Bulleid 'West Country' Class Pacific No.34008 *Padstow* is depicted in the evening sunshine near Upper Warlingham hauling the 4.40pm London Bridge to Brighton train on 7th June 1962. It is recorded that *Padstow* was a regular performer on Brighton to London (and vice versa) trains at this time. Brighton shed's allocation of these locomotives had increased from five to nine during early 1962 and it presumably had more than enough engines to cover the available work, hence the appearance of a Bulleid locomotive on this comparatively easy duty. The days of steam on the Oxted Line were drawing to a close at the time this picture was taken, however, due to the introduction of diesel units and scenes such as this were soon to be confined to history. *Padstow* achieved a degree of fame when it became the first rebuilt Bulleid Pacific to be allocated to Brighton shed in November 1960. *Les Dench*

Riddlesdown viaduct carries the Oxted Line over a quarry and its associated installations, and in this picture the passing train is almost totally lost in the smoke and steam emanating from the industrial premises and BR Standard Class 4MT 2-6-4T No.80016. The train depicted is the 9.08am Victoria to Tunbridge Wells West and this remarkable shot was taken on 10th March 1962. *John Beckett*

The North Downs, with their distinctive chalk 'scar', provide the backdrop to this picture which shows SECR H class 0-4-4T No.31533 waiting to leave Oxted with a train to Tunbridge Wells on 7th June 1962. The railway reached this town on 10th March 1884 when the SER and LBSCR opened their jointly owned line from South Croydon. This line continued to East Grinstead, the section beyond Crowhurst being solely owned by the latter company. In 1881 the nominally independent Oxted & Groombridge Company was incorporated to build the 12 miles-long stretch from Hurst Green Junction to Ashurst Junction, on the East Grinstead to Tunbridge Wells line, and this opened throughout on 1st October 1888. *Les Dench*

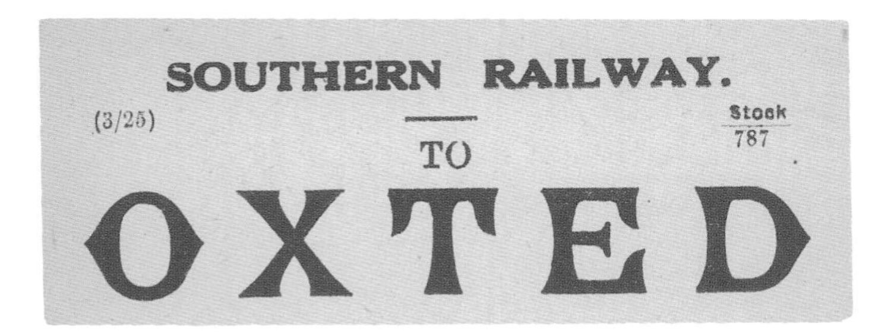

When the original promoters opened their line they probably did not anticipate that heavy commuter traffic would develop in this Surrey 'stockbroker belt' territory. In the late 1950s Hurst Green Halt, just south of Oxted, was a ramshackle wooden station overdue for improvement and BR replaced it with a compact but modern station with much longer concrete platforms, on a different site. Part of the new up platform is visible in this photograph with a substantial BR sign informing people that a new station was on its way. Construction commenced in 1959, but the gestation period appears to have been prolonged because it did not open until June 1961, from which time the old station was closed. *Colour-Rail.com*

South of Oxted, the Tunbridge Wells line served a string of villages in addition to the fairly large town of Edenbridge which also has a station on the Redhill to Tonbridge line. Here, an Oxted-bound 'pull-push' service with H Class No.31522 in charge pauses at Hever on 7th June 1962. At the time of this picture this small station appears to be in quite respectable condition complete with a substantial footbridge, gentlemen's toilet and platform oil lamps. Note the signal box on the down platform; it must have been a bit unnerving and distracting for the signalman if children peered inquisitively through the windows when a train was due. *Les Dench*

A picture taken near Cowden on 27th October 1962, showing a Tunbridge Wells West to Oxted train shuffling along behind SECR H Class No.31518. Note the massive embankment built to carry the railway – that must have been a huge civil engineering operation at a time prior to mechanisation when navvies still performed most of the work. This picture gives an idea of the truly rural nature of the line south of Edenbridge. *John Beckett*

No.31518 is seen again, propelling an Oxted to Tunbridge Wells train near Cowden in 1962. These trains were worked on the 'pull-push' basis with only the fireman on the footplate of the locomotive when propelling, the driver being in a cab at the front from where he controlled the train. No.31518 was constructed at Ashford works emerging in July 1909; this locomotive survived to become one of the last three survivors in service, being withdrawn from Three Bridges shed in January 1964. *John Beckett*

Autumn is often a rewarding time for the railway photographer with cooler days and softer light, conditions that are exemplified here by this shot of an unidentified H Class tank locomotive pulling away from Ashurst with a train bound for Tunbridge Wells on 29th September 1962. Note how the photographer has timed his shot perfectly and pressed the shutter just before the engine reached the dark shadow created by the trees. Ashurst station can be glimpsed in the background. This view has changed dramatically during the ensuing years and mature trees have sprung up quite close to the tracks. Remarkable though it may seem, at one time Ashurst was the point at which the 4.48pm Victoria to Brighton/Tunbridge Wells West train divided, the front portion being taken forward by the train engine while a second locomotive, which had been waiting in the goods yard, took the rear section on to Tunbridge Wells. *John Beckett*

A delightful rural scene. The crew of H Class No.31544 have certainly ensured that they had sufficient coal to get them to Oxted and back: note that the bunker is filled to capacity! These locomotives had a 'pagoda' cab which provided additional protection for the enginemen. In this June 1963 picture another 'pull-push' train is depicted, this time leaving Groombridge station, the platforms of which can just be seen beyond the overbridge. At the time of this photograph the section of line between Groombridge and Tunbridge Wells West was a very busy stretch of track due to the fact that four rural lines converged on Groombridge and up to four trains every hour in each direction could sometimes be seen – a spotter's paradise! One by one these routes fell victim to the dreaded Beeching axe and today only the trains of the Spa Valley Railway come this way. *Martin Smith*

An Oxted to Tunbridge Wells West train is propelled towards its destination by an unidentified H Class 0-4-4T on a bright and sunny 5th March 1960. Note that the train is formed of an elderly pre-grouping 'pull-push' set in crimson livery rather than the Maunsell coaches seen in previous illustrations in this part of the book. This picture was taken near the site of High Rocks Halt which took its name from a picturesque outcrop of sandstone rocks atop a woodland ridge in the adjacent Broadwater forest. The halt, a rather basic wooden structure, opened in 1907, suffered a temporary wartime closure from October 1939 to June 1942, and was shut permanently from 5th May 1952. *John Langford*

The 1960s Beeching closures hit the east Sussex branches hard, with both the Three Bridges to Tunbridge Wells West and 'Cuckoo' lines being closed completely, and even the Brighton to Tunbridge Wells section was severed in 1969 between Lewes and Uckfield due to the condition of the viaduct at Lewes. In 1985 the link from Eridge to Tunbridge Wells Central was also closed leaving the long, rural secondary line from Oxted to Uckfield *in situ* mainly for the benefit of commuters. One of the largest towns served by this route is Crowborough and in this illustration LBSCR K Class 'Mogul' No.32340 is pictured shunting there on 25th March 1961. The signal box and station seem to have been repainted just prior to the photographer's visit(!) and everything looks creditably spick and span. It is sad to consider that at the time of this photograph Crowborough had a regular service of trains to Tonbridge and London, and Bulleid Pacifics, 'Schools' Class 4-4-0s, Maunsell 'Moguls' plus a range of BR Standard classes were a regular sight in addition to the lovely K Class locomotives. How times have changed! *John Beckett*

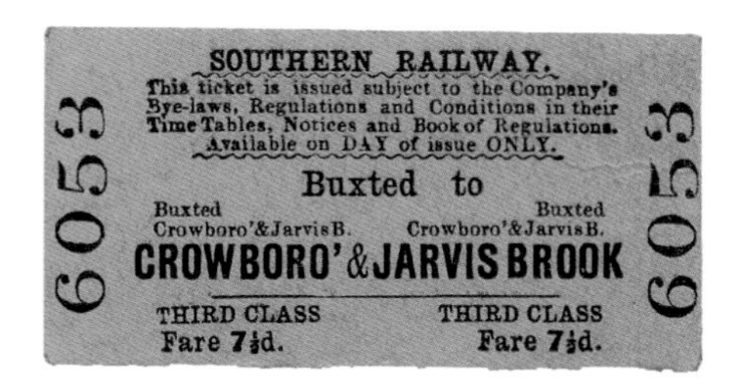

BR Standard Class 4MT 2-6-4T No.80035 exerts a mighty effort as it gets away from Eridge with the 10.38am Victoria to Brighton via Oxted train on 17th March 1962. No.80035 was based at Watford in the 1950s, and moved to Ashford when displaced by electrification. In early May 1962 it was transferred from Ashford to Exmouth Junction shed and the author can find no record of this engine ever being based on the Central Section of the SR. It is possible that it was 'borrowed' by Brighton shed whilst in the course of moving to the West Country so this is likely to be a very rare shot of this locomotive at work in Sussex. The 10.38am train from Victoria is advertised in the 1957 timetable as calling at only the principal stations to Eridge and then all stations to Brighton, except Falmer. *John Beckett*

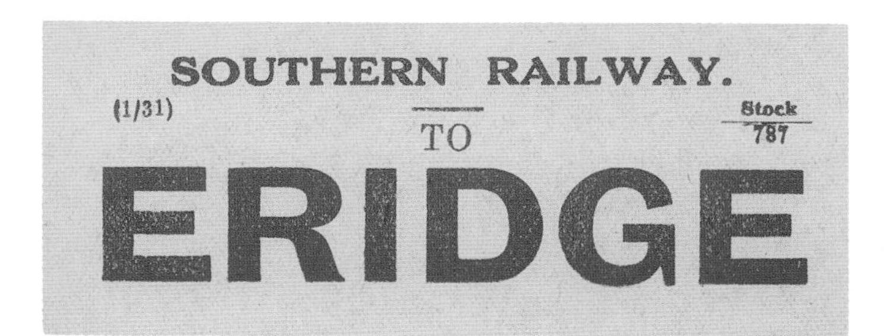
SOUTHERN RAILWAY.
(1/31) TO Stock 787
ERIDGE

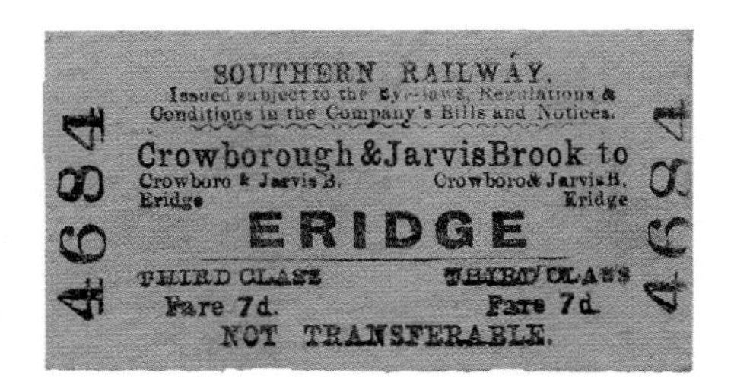
SOUTHERN RAILWAY.
Issued subject to the Bye-laws, Regulations & Conditions in the Company's Bills and Notices.
4684 Crowborough & Jarvis Brook to 4684
Crowboro & Jarvis B. Eridge | Crowboro & Jarvis B. Eridge
ERIDGE
THIRD CLASS Fare 7d. | THIRD CLASS Fare 7d.
NOT TRANSFERABLE.

A Brighton to Tonbridge train is seen near the site of High Rocks Halt, between Groombridge and Tunbridge Wells West, on 13th May 1961. Maunsell 'Mogul' No.31407, hauling a Maunsell 4-set of coaches, provides the motive power. Note the LBSCR whistle board. The border between East Sussex and Kent crosses the line at this point and the train appears to have just entered the latter county, but some of the trees in the distance are likely to be in Sussex. *John Beckett*

In the 1840s the port of Lewes was in steady decline and the Brighton, Lewes & Hastings Railway Co. considered that the small port of Newhaven was capable of development. The local company was taken over by the LBSCR in 1845 but the 'Brighton' company pressed ahead with a proposal to build a branch from Lewes to Newhaven and this opened on 8th December 1847. Newhaven was confidently expected to become a great port and a guide book of 1852 referred to the 'Liverpool of the South'. The port remained tidal, however, and improvements commenced in 1878 following the creation of the Newhaven Harbour Company. Moles were built together with a quay for packets and a quayside station and, on the west side of the river Ouse, a tramway was laid in connection with the works. Fixed sailings began on 1st April 1889. The extension to Seaford, 2½ miles to the east, was opened on 1st June 1864. The Seaford branch was electrified in July 1935 so it is not surprising that colour images of steam operations are far from plentiful. The legendary 'Brighton' Atlantics were associated with Newhaven boat train workings for many years and this picture was taken on 13th April 1958, the very last time an engine of this class visited the town. By that time No.32424 *Beachy Head* was the sole survivor of the class and facing imminent withdrawal, so the Railway Correspondence & Travel Society (RCTS) organised the 'Brighton Atlantic Farewell' rail tour which was hauled by No.32424 from Victoria to Newhaven. This picture shows *Beachy Head* simmering on Newhaven shed alongside BR Standard Class 4MT tank locomotive No.80154, the last engine built at Brighton works, which later took the participants along the coast to Brighton from where they returned to London behind a 'King Arthur' Class engine. A few days after this picture was taken No.32424 took a train of empty stock from Lancing works to Micheldever and retired to Eastleigh works whence it never returned. A tragic end to an outstanding class. *Derek Penney*

The Kemp Town branch was just over a mile long and left the East Coast Line at Kemp Town Junction which was situated a mile or so outside Brighton station on the Lewes line. The branch opened for business on 2nd August 1869, but it was a circuitous route and in 1906 a half-hourly rail-motor service was introduced to meet stiff competition from electric tram cars. The branch was closed to passengers for a period during the First World War during which time passengers found alternative means of transport and never returned to the railway. The result was that closure was inevitable and this occurred from 2nd January 1933; however the line stayed open for goods traffic until the early 1970s. The branch may not have been very long but its short length was more than compensated for by two viaducts, one of which boasted 14 arches, and the 1,024 yards-long Kemp Town tunnel – one shudders to think of the construction cost per mile. There were even two intermediate stations, one of which, Hartington Road Halt, was only open from January 1906 to April 1911. Most colour pictures taken on the branch in its dying days tended to be artificial rail tours which were hardly typical of normal operations, but here is an everyday scene showing beautifully clean LBSCR E4 Class 0-6-2T No.32503 shunting at Kemp Town goods depot on 14th April 1962. Note the shunter carrying his pole which he used to 'unhook' wagons from each other and to couple them. A far cry from modern practice. *Les Dench*

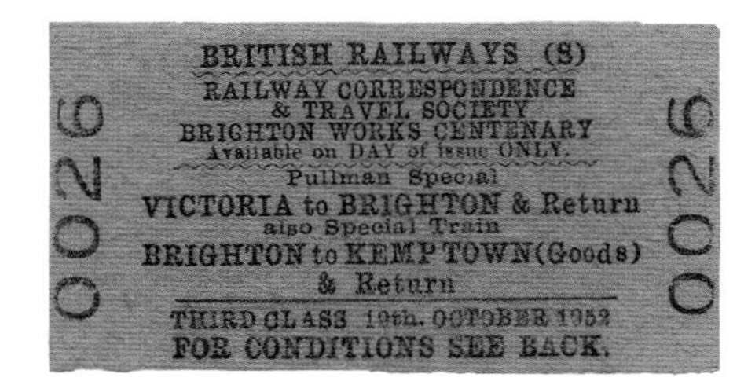

In the author's view the Brighton to Horsham route, or Steyning Line as it was generally called by local people, was the least appealing of the Sussex branches, perhaps because it was double track which gave it the appearance of a secondary line rather than a branch. In addition, the scenery on the line was not outstanding nor were there any notable gradients. It was also known as the 'Linger and Die Line'. The route was opened in two stages, the first from Shoreham-by-Sea to Partridge Green on 1st July 1861, while the remaining stretch on to Horsham (Itchingfield Junction) carried its first passengers on 16th September of the same year. Steyning was the most important town served by the route and in this portrait Ivatt-designed Class 2MT 2-6-2T No.41314 stands in the station's up platform with a Horsham train in tow on 30th April 1964, just a few days before steam was ousted. This class was new to the Steyning Line and this particular engine was based in Devon prior to coming to Sussex. In October 1961 the line's centenary was marked by a special train hauled by LBSCR E4 Class No.32468 and the station seen here was the venue for local celebrations which had the former Brighton works 'Terrier' No.32635 as their centrepiece. Doubtless an altogether different atmosphere was evident when the line was closed, apart from a short stub to Beeding cement works, in March 1966. *Les Dench*

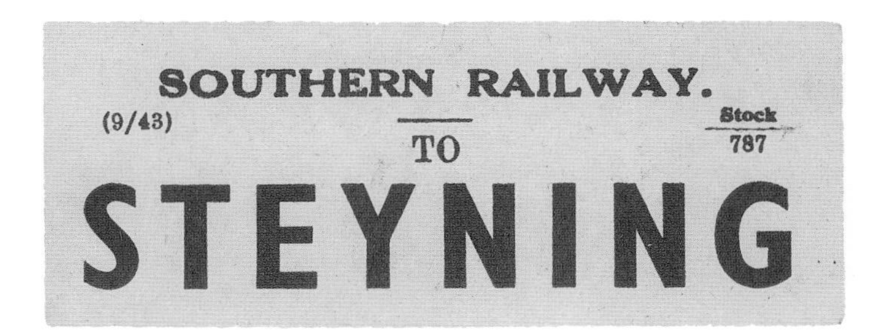
SOUTHERN RAILWAY.
(9/43) Stock 787
TO
STEYNING

2nd - SINGLE SINGLE - 2nd
8040 8040
Bramber to
Bramber Steyning Bramber Steyning
STEYNING
(S) 3d. Fare 3d. (S)
For conditions see over For conditions see over

West Grinstead was almost totally isolated from even small centres of population and had a delightful rural air, apart from the rumble of traffic on the main Haywards Heath to Billingshurst road which was carried over the railway on a bridge located immediately south of the station. Most unusually for a station on this line the main buildings were located above the tracks at road level. When this picture was taken of Ivatt tank locomotive No.41326 standing in the up platform with a Horsham-bound train on a delightful day in 1963 the decline in the line's fortunes is already in evidence – note the overgrown siding in the foreground indicating that the goods yard had already been closed. Like No.41314 depicted in the previous illustration, No.41326 was also an interloper, having been allocated to Skipton and Bradford (Manningham) sheds earlier in its career. Note also the comfortable BR Standard 3-set of coaches forming the train which was identical to some of the stock used on Waterloo to Weymouth expresses! *Gerald Daniels*

Further signs that the line's fortunes were ebbing away are provided by this picture taken at West Grinstead on 30th April 1964. This view is looking northwards towards Horsham and shows that the signal box has apparently been taken out of use and the signal arms removed. Certainly, there is no sign of any life in the box! Bunker-first Ivatt 2-6-2T No.41299 is seen entering the station on a train bound for Brighton. One wonders how many passengers were waiting to board. Diesel multiple units took over from steam just a few days after this scene was recorded and six weeks later regular steam working was banished from the Brighton area after a mere 123 years. *Les Dench*

This picture shows Ivatt 2-6-2T No.41324 heading northwards at Partridge Green on 9th June 1962. This engine was another infiltrator to Sussex and before arriving at Brighton shed had previously been allocated to Bangor, Birkenhead, Rhyl and Warrington (Dallam) depots on the London Midland Region. The station here was really quite pretty with the stationmaster's house, passenger accommodation, goods shed and signal box all situated on, or adjacent to, the southbound platform. There were also shrubs on the platforms which enhanced the appeal of the station. The 1957 summer timetable listed around a dozen trains each way on the route on weekdays with seven on Sundays, the weekday service being supplemented by one or two short workings between Brighton and Steyning only. The summer 1961 timetable advertised as many as sixteen down and seventeen up weekday trains – a very generous service. Prior to the coming of the Ivatt tank locomotives, M7 Class 0-4-4Ts and E4 Class 0-6-2Ts could be found on passenger workings while goods traffic was powered by C2X 0-6-0s and K Class 'Moguls'. *Les Dench*

2nd - SINGLE SINGLE 2nd

2984

West Grinstead to

West Grinstead West Grinstead
Partridge Green Partridge Green

PARTRIDGE GREEN

(S) FARE (S)

For condit'ns see over For condit'ns see over

2984

SOUTHERN RAILWAY.

(10/24) Stock 787

TO

PARTRIDGE GREEN

The branch line from Pulborough to Petworth was originally built as part of the Mid-Sussex Railway's single track Horsham to Petworth line which opened on 10th October 1859 and was the first railway in this part of the county. The line was extended southwards from Pulborough (Hardham Junction) to Arundel Junction on 3rd August 1863, with doubling of the line from Horsham to Hardham coinciding with the opening of the extension. The branch to Petworth was extended to Midhurst, this section opening on 15th October 1866, where it met the LSWR line from Petersfield which had opened for traffic in September 1864. The Pulborough to Petersfield line ran through a particularly attractive part of rural Sussex and Hampshire, but one that was sparsely populated and hardly fertile territory for the railway. Passenger services were abandoned on the entire line from 7th February 1955, with the section beyond Midhurst being closed completely. The Pulborough to Midhurst stretch remained open for goods traffic, however, and became a favourite destination for rail tour operators and in this shot LBSCR E4 Class No.32503 is seen piloting E6 Class No.32417 on the LCGB's 'Sussex Coast Limited' rail tour on 24th June 1962. The former Selham station building is just visible in the background but apart from that there are few other buildings to be seen. *John Beckett*

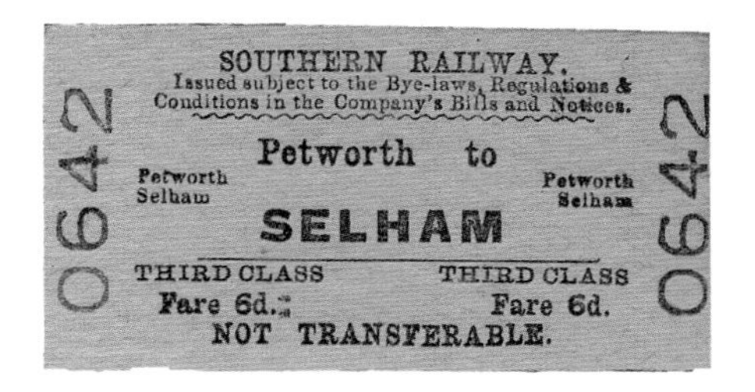

0642

SOUTHERN RAILWAY.
Issued subject to the Bye-laws, Regulations & Conditions in the Company's Bills and Notices.

Petworth to

Petworth Selham | Petworth Selham

SELHAM

THIRD CLASS | THIRD CLASS
Fare 6d. | Fare 6d.

NOT TRANSFERABLE.

0642

A sad day at Midhurst. The authorities decided that goods traffic on the Petworth to Midhurst section was insufficient to justify the line's retention and it was closed in October 1964. The closure was commemorated by the joint LCGB/RCTS 'Midhurst Belle' rail tour which is depicted entering Midhurst behind Maunsell Q Class 0-6-0 No.30530 on 18th October. In addition to visiting Midhurst, which was obviously the main purpose of the trip, the participants were treated to a run down the Guildford to Horsham line, a journey along the short Kemp Town branch and a high speed run from Brighton to Victoria behind steam in the unusual form of Bulleid 'Merchant Navy' Pacific No.35007 *Aberdeen Commonwealth.* What a wonderful day out and one that will never be repeated! *Ian Wright*

9173 3rd-SINGLE SINGLE-3rd 9173
Midhurst to
Midhurst Midhurst
Petersfield Petersfield
PETERSFIELD
(S) 1/6H FARE 1/6H (S)
For Conditions see over For Conditions see over

Railway aficionados loved the sleepy, tranquil atmosphere of the Horsham to Guildford line, but the empty seats in the train seen here tell their own story – the line was hopelessly unremunerative and probably never paid its way at any time in its life. This delightful scenic byway was built by the Horsham & Guildford Direct Railway Company, which was a very impressive name for a small company endeavouring to construct this somewhat unimportant route. The Company was incorporated in 1860 and, after negotiating with both the LSWR and LBSCR, sold its uncompleted works to the latter in 1864. The line was opened on 2nd October 1865 and led an uneventful existence until total closure came on 14th June 1965, so the route just missed its centenary. Even in the 1930s, when private motor transport was still in its infancy as far as the ordinary citizen was concerned, a meagre service of eight weekday through trains was advertised, with some short workings from Guildford to Cranleigh, the only significant intermediate centre of population served. Judging by the overgrown siding in the yard on the right, goods facilities had already been withdrawn when this shot was taken in 1963. The picture shows trains crossing at Baynards, a station much more famous for its outstanding floral displays than the frequency of its train service. Indeed, such was the station's fame as a horticultural centre that visitors came from far and wide to admire the fine displays of dahlias but, predictably, rarely arrived by train and contributed nothing to the railway's finances apart from the purchase of the occasional platform ticket. The locomotive in view is Ivatt 2-6-2T No.41327, a one-time resident of Skipton shed, which arrived on the SR in the early 1960s. *Gerald Daniels*

Bognor Regis – a Mecca for the steam enthusiast? The short 3½ miles-long branch from Barnham to Bognor Regis is rather featureless and unlikely to have attracted many steam photographers, but here is a view of smartly turned-out LBSCR K Class 'Mogul' No.32353 simmering at the platform end with a rail tour on 24th June 1962. The special train is the LCGB's 'Sussex Coast Limited' which was powered by the 'Mogul' from Pulborough to Bognor Regis and then on to Haywards Heath where preserved LSWR T9 Class 4-4-0 No.120 took over. Prior to electrification Bognor had a small steam locomotive depot adjacent to the easternmost platform, the original wooden building dated from the 1860s, but this was replaced by the LBSCR in 1903 by a two-road brick-built shed which remained intact, despite the decline in its importance following electrification, until it was closed in 1953 and partially demolished in 1956. No.32353 had obviously had to turn on the turntable so this vital piece of equipment remained in use well after the shed's closure as an operational depot. Despite receiving a general repair at Eastleigh works in 1961 this elegant machine was unceremoniously withdrawn for accountancy reasons at the end of 1962 together with its sister locomotives. *Colour-Rail.com*

The 1¾ miles-long Hampton Court branch is one of the few branch lines in the London suburban area to feature in this album. It was opened by the LSWR on 1st February 1849 and electrified as early as 1916, being included in the first LSWR electrification scheme. Thus steam locomotives became a rarity at a very early date and the tiny steam engine shed was taken out of use, although steam engines occasionally worked excursions conveying visitors to the palace. The lack of a turntable at Hampton Court deterred steam rail tour organisers, but on 16th December 1962 the joint RCTS/SLS 'South West Suburban' tour visited the branch utilising a couple of veteran Beattie well tank locomotives, Nos.30585 and 30587, coupled bunker to bunker which obviated the need for bunker-first running. In this portrait the pair are seen leaving Hampton Court with great gusto, or at least as much gusto as these diminutive engines could muster. Built by Beyer Peacock & Co. Ltd as long ago as 1874, these locomotives were originally constructed for LSWR suburban services so it really was a case of *déjà vu*. Incredible though it may seem, most members of this class were withdrawn from traffic between 1888 and 1898 and the machines seen here were two of a trio of these lovely little engines specially retained to work the Wadebridge to Wenfordbridge mineral line in Cornwall, which had severe curvature and weight restrictions. The end came for these locomotives in the summer of 1962 when Great Western Railway 0-6-0PT No.1368 passed clearance tests on various lines worked by the Beattie engines and a further batch of locomotives of the same class was drafted to Wadebridge to replace them. It seems remarkable that these two locomotives, which were moved to Eastleigh following their displacement, were able to work a farewell tour more than 70 years after the first of their sister engines was withdrawn from service. *Martin Smith*

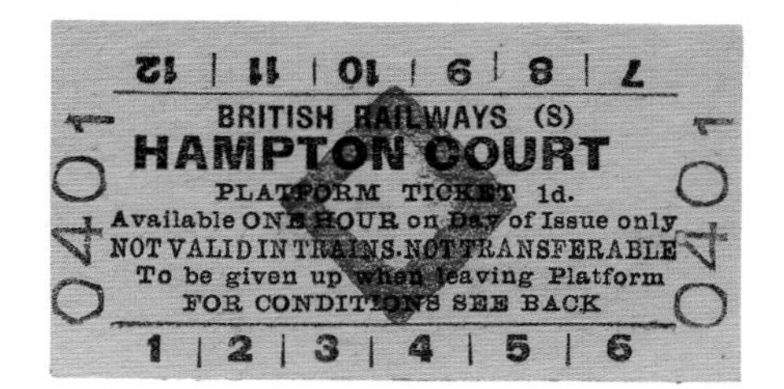

When asked to nominate his favourite SR branch line, the average railway enthusiast is unlikely to consider the Bordon branch; the Lyme Regis, Hayling Island and 'Cuckoo' lines are sure to be rated highly, but not the Bentley to Bordon line. The branch was designed primarily to handle military traffic from the nearby Woolmer Forest, and other camps in the area, and constructed under a Light Railway Order granted to the LSWR in October 1902. This meant that it was built with ungated level crossings and construction proceeded rapidly across the largely flat terrain, the line opening for business on 11th December 1905. The station building at Bordon was rather basic and constructed in what could be vaguely described as 'Colonel Stephens' light railway style' using corrugated iron supported on steel framing. The structure was extended in 1916 in order to cope with the very heavy military traffic it handled at that time. Remarkably, at its zenith Bordon station consisted of four platforms each able to accommodate ten-coach trains and on some occasions, especially during the First World War, the branch's advertised public passenger service had to be suspended so priority could be given to military trains. This appears to have been the line's heyday and by the 1930s army traffic was declining. Latterly, a two-coach 'pull-push' train sufficed for the local customers and even this traffic ebbed away with the inevitable result that services were withdrawn from 16th September 1957. The branch remained open for the remaining military traffic, however, and this enabled enthusiasts to travel over it on rail tours that were arranged from time to time. In this view photographers vie for the best position as Maunsell 'Mogul' No.31639 stands at a snowy Bordon station while working the Bordon branch section of the LCGB's 'S15 Commemorative' rail tour on 16th January 1966. Later, participants were treated to a rousing run over the steeply-graded Mid Hants line with the 'Mogul' assisting S15 Class 4-6-0 No.30837. *Roy Hobbs*

2nd-SINGLE.SINGLE-2nd

8689

Bentley to

Bentley Bordon | Bentley Bordon

BORDON

(S) 10d. FARE 10d. (S)

For conditions see over For conditions see over

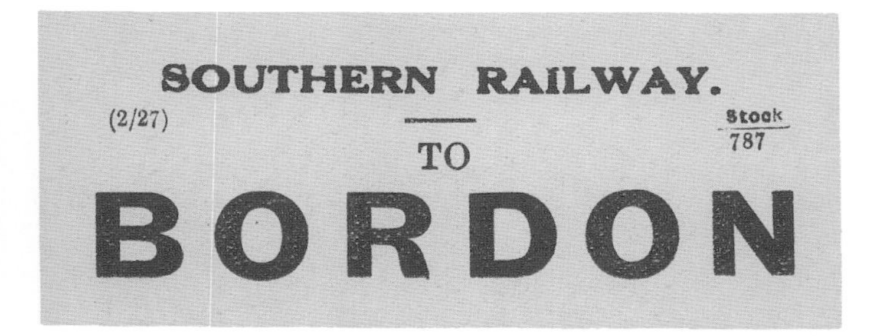

SOUTHERN RAILWAY.

(2/27) | Stock 787

TO

BORDON

On 4th November 1963 Hampshire lost one its best-loved lines, the 4½ miles-long branch from Havant to Hayling Island, a true holiday-makers' line. It was proposed by the Hayling Railway Company which obtained its Act in July 1860 but the company made the disastrous decision to take the line along the western shore of the island which involved reclaiming part of Langston Harbour mudflats. The 'reclaimed' land was quickly claimed back by the sea which carried away spoil almost as fast as it was deposited. A more practical course was eventually found and the line was opened on 17th July 1867. Sadly, the line was vulnerable to closure due to the seasonal nature of its traffic and closure was authorised by the government in 1963. Owing to severe weight restrictions on Langston bridge the only locomotives permitted over the line were LBSCR A1X Class 0-6-0Ts, commonly known as 'Terriers', and in this shot No.32636 is seen waiting to leave Havant with the last train over the line on Sunday 3rd November 1963, a LCGB rail tour from London. The final public trains had operated the previous day, because by this time there was no winter Sunday service over the branch. The coach immediately behind the engine is No.S1000S, an experimental glass-fibre bodied vehicle constructed at Eastleigh on a surplus underframe. *Martin Smith*

Members of the British Railways Board probably considered that their jobs caused anxiety and unease but, in reality, one of the most stressful jobs on BR at that time was the post of crossing keeper at Langston. One wonders how the remuneration compared to that paid to the Board members! In the summer months a frequent service operated on the Hayling Island line and the gates were often shut against traffic on the adjacent main road and long jams resulted. Perhaps the staff at Langston got used to the abusive comments by irate motorists who had been caught up in the queues. In this illustration a long line of cars can just be discerned on the road as A1X Class No.32678 enters Langston station with a train bound for Hayling Island in June 1963. The crossing keeper's cabin is partially visible on the left while on the right the original 'Brighton' running-in board can be seen. *Martin Smith*

Langston bridge was the only engineering work of any consequence on the branch and in this shot 'Terrier' No.32646 rumbles across with a two-coach train in the early 1960s. Note that the engine sports a spark arrester designed to prevent lineside fires and protect the bridge timbers. The concrete bases of the timbers were a relatively recent feature, being added by the Southern Railway in the 1930s. The bridge's deteriorating condition caused BR to seek closure which resulted in the line losing its services in November 1963, as previously mentioned. The photographer, who was a professional railwayman at the time, presumably had a lineside pass enabling him to walk along the track and this picture appears to have been taken from the signal box conveniently located adjacent to the bridge's opening span. *Gerald Daniels*

Dark clouds hide the setting sun and produce a memorable reflection as a two-coach train crosses Langston bridge and heads for Havant on 16th March 1963. What a pity the engine was not making any smoke to add life to the shot. *John Beckett*

Big coach, little engine. LBSCR 'Terrier' No.32678 is dwarfed by the coaches it is hauling but, despite their lack of stature, these sprightly locomotives had a good reputation among enginemen and were capable of a power output out of all proportion to their size. Note the wooden platform at North Hayling survived until closure together with a rudimentary waiting shelter. The tiny halt here would have looked much different to the structure depicted if the ideas of the LBSCR had come to fruition. In 1900 it drew up plans for the total rebuilding of the station; this involved doubling the length of the platforms and enlarging the station building which was to be rebuilt in brick with the usual facilities. Presumably it was anticipated that there would be considerable residential development in the immediate vicinity, but this failed to materialise. This picture, which shows a down train, was taken on 24th April 1962. *Derek Penney*

No.32678 is seen again, this time near North Hayling with a train for Hayling Island on 15th July 1962. This shot gives a good idea of the flat terrain through which the line passed and its close proximity to the sea – note the boat on the left. This engine was one of the 'younger' members of the A1X Class and appeared from Brighton works in July 1880. It was withdrawn in 1925, but subsequently reinstated and despatched to the Isle of Wight where it gave yeoman service for 17 years before being returned to the mainland. It was finally withdrawn in October 1963, but survived into preservation after leading a very charmed life. *Alan Reeve*

After deciding on Hayling Island as the location of their summer break it is unlikely that holiday-makers would want to take a trip to Lincoln or even Salisbury, but maybe these posters were aimed at the local population who may have been more amenable. *Stuart Ackley collection*

SOUTHERN RAILWAY.

(11/38) TO Stock 787

HAYLING ISLAND

Hayling Island station was known as South Hayling until it was renamed on 1st July 1892. The station was built with fancy herringbone pattern brickwork but this was soon covered with red tiles which offered greater protection from the elements. Note that there was also a bay platform in addition to the one seen here, but it was used only at the height of the summer holiday traffic. In times past there was a small engine shed here but it was closed in 1894 and subsequently demolished; the coaling stage, however, remained in use until the end. This picture was taken a few weeks before closure, on 17th October 1963. *Stuart Ackley collection*

The history of the Alton to Winchester line can be traced as far back as 1845 when the LSWR surveyed the countryside between the towns with a view to building a railway, but this idea came to nothing. Fifteen years later the Alton, Alresford & Winchester Railway Company revived the scheme, which was widely supported, and it came as no surprise when it obtained its Act on 28th June 1861. Construction commenced in 1863 and the line was opened on 2nd October 1865. The line was worked by the LSWR from the outset, the initial service consisting of four weekday trains between Guildford and Southampton Terminus. The start of the line's decline can be traced back to the commencement of electric trains between Alton and Waterloo in 1937, from which time the Mid Hants line lost its through London trains. The introduction of diesel units on Mid Hants services in 1957 brought an increase in passenger numbers but, even so, the route was listed for closure in the Beeching Report of 1963. An epic struggle followed between local people who wanted to retain their service and the monolithic BR which was accused of publishing misleading information about the line's finances. It was a sad day when, on 25th August 1971, the government gave approval for closure and the last BR trains ran on 4th February 1973. The controversy sparked by BR's proposals led to the formation of a preservation group and, thanks to the untiring efforts of members of the Mid Hants Railway, it is still possible to make the fascinating journey from Alton to Alresford with steam traction. During its twilight years the line was used as a diversionary route for Bournemouth Line expresses and here the 10.30am Waterloo to Bournemouth train is seen ascending Medstead bank behind Bulleid Pacific No.34021 *Dartmoor* on 12th June 1966. Like many locomotives at that time, No.34021 appears to be in a parlous condition and struggling on the heavy 1 in 60 gradient. *Roy Hobbs*

While the decision to shut the line was regrettable, with one exception all of the original Mid Hants stations remain open today on the preserved section and are lovingly maintained. Itchen Abbas station, however, was located west of Alresford and, therefore, is not part of today's Mid Hants line. It was the quietest of all the line's intermediate stations and merely served two small villages. It was originally known as Itchen Abbotts and was built with a signal box and passing loop but these fell victim to an economy drive by the Southern Railway in 1931. The goods yard was closed in 1962 and the last member of the station staff was pensioned off in 1965. This portrait of this quiet country station was taken on 2nd July 1967. *Stuart Ackley collection*

The origins of the Fawley branch can be traced back to the turn of the century when the LSWR obtained a Light Railway Order to build a line from Totton down the western shore of Southampton Water. Construction was deferred until the early 1920s, however, the route eventually opening on 20th July 1926, by which time the LSWR had become part of the Southern Railway. It was a very circuitous route for passengers travelling from Southampton and the vast majority continued to use the Hythe ferry, with the result that passenger traffic along the branch was insignificant. The 1957 summer timetable advertised an unbalanced service on weekdays consisting of two down trains and three in the reverse direction, the trains no doubt being timed to coincide with the workers' shifts at the adjacent oil refinery. There was only one train in each direction on Sundays. Not surprisingly, the line's career as a passenger railway was very brief and the service, such as it was, was withdrawn from 14th February 1966. Oil and military traffic remains buoyant, however, and it seems to have a very secure future albeit as a goods only line. The sparse passenger service did little to attract photographers and colour pictures of ordinary steam-hauled trains are rare, but here is a view of the signalman at Marchwood holding up the single line tablet as the LCGB's 'Hampshire Branch Lines' rail tour approaches. The locomotives are a pair of USA Class engines, Nos.30064 and 30069, and this picture was taken on 9th April 1967. *John Beckett*

Judging by the long platform the railway authorities were optimistic that the Fawley branch would attract many passengers and be a money spinner for them – alas! In this photograph USA Class locomotive Nos.30073 and 30064 pose at Fawley at the head of the RCTS 'Solent' rail tour on 20th March 1966. The oil installations in the background may not be pretty but at least the refinery has ensured the line's survival. *Roy Hobbs*

The single track branch from Lymington Junction, west of Brockenhurst, to the port of Lymington was proposed by the Lymington Railway Company and opened on 12th July 1858. The port was used by ferries to and from the Isle of Wight and the local company anticipated an increase in trade, but the LSWR initially took little interest, focussing instead on its Portsmouth to Isle of Wight service. The LSWR's attitude changed in 1878 following its takeover of the local Lymington Company and an extension from Lymington Town station to the pier was opened on 1st May 1884, the ferries also being taken over by the LSWR in the same year. Just before the Second World War the Southern Railway introduced a 'drive on, drive off' car ferry service between Lymington and Yarmouth, one of the first of its kind. In more recent years the branch became noteworthy as one of the last refuges of the M7 Class 0-4-4Ts which lasted until May 1964, by which time the survivors were well past their best. This illustration provides a comprehensive view of Lymington Town station and depicts a train leaving towards Brockenhurst on 31st May 1963 behind an unidentified M7 Class locomotive. At that time the station retained its overall roof, complete with rather peculiar smoke vents, and was semaphore signalled. Note the tiny engine shed on the right of the shot which dated from the opening in 1858. There was no turntable provided because the line was normally worked by tank engines, but one was available at nearby Brockenhurst. *Stuart Ackley collection*

Photographed on a damp day in August 1966, BR Standard Class 4MT 2-6-4T No.80032 negotiates the tight curve at the approach to Lymington Town station with a train for Brockenhurst. The train comprises a Bulleid-designed 3-set of coaches. Note the rather dainty lower quadrant signals and gas lamp. These locomotives, supplemented by Ivatt-designed 2-6-2Ts, were staple motive power on the branch for the final three years of steam traction following the displacement of the M7s. *Stuart Ackley collection*

The old order on the Lymington branch. The Drummond M7 Class monopolised services on the branch for many years and in this portrait No.30480, which is in creditably clean condition, is seen leaving Lymington Pier with a train to Brockenhurst on 19th August 1961. The coach immediately behind the engine is one of the notoriously uncomfortable SECR ten-compartment third vehicles which had very hard seats. The passengers would 'have had enough' by the time the train reached Brockenhurst! Note that every piece of fixed railway property in the picture appears to have been newly painted. This was BR's last steam-worked passenger branch line, where steam traction lasted until 3rd April 1967. *John Beckett*

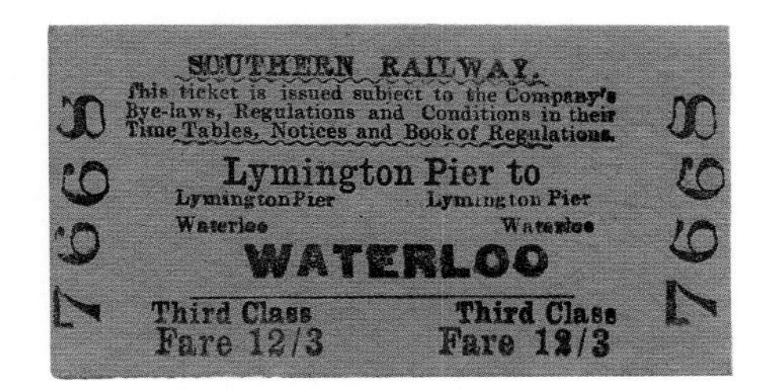

A real rural backwater. Daggons Road station on 6th Juy 1961, and Maunsell 'Mogul' No.31404, working the 5.32pm goods from Wimborne to Salisbury East Yard, is almost lost in the shadows. The tiny station here was originally known as 'Daggens Road', however, the nearest settlement to the station was actually Alderholt, Daggons being further to the west. The small signal box, on the right of the picture, was once a block post but this was reduced in status to a ground frame only, in 1934. The photographer comments that, owing to the nature of the restricted layout, tow roping of wagons may have been authorised at this location. *John Langford*

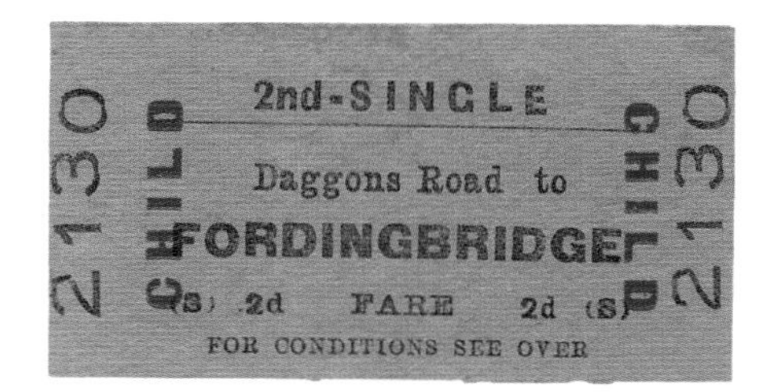

In addition to its regular service of local trains between Bournemouth and Brockenhurst/Salisbury, this line had a number of odd workings that only operated during the summer holiday season and in the summer 1957 timetable Saturday-only through trains from Cardiff to New Milton and Swansea to Bournemouth are advertised. One would have thought that it would have been quicker to route these over the Somerset & Dorset line but perhaps pathways were not available. The identity of this train is something of a mystery but judging by the headcode it is a train from Salisbury to Bournemouth West which had presumably been specially strengthened for day trippers to the coast. This picture shows Maunsell 'Mogul' No.31632 pulling away from Broadstone on 7th September 1962; the line on the left leads to Hamworthy Junction. *John Beckett*

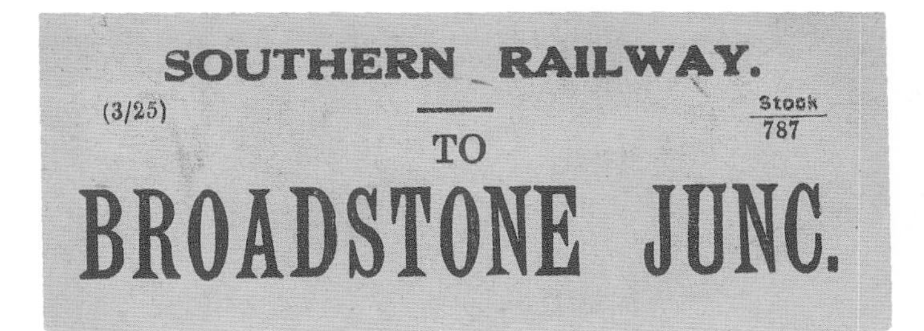

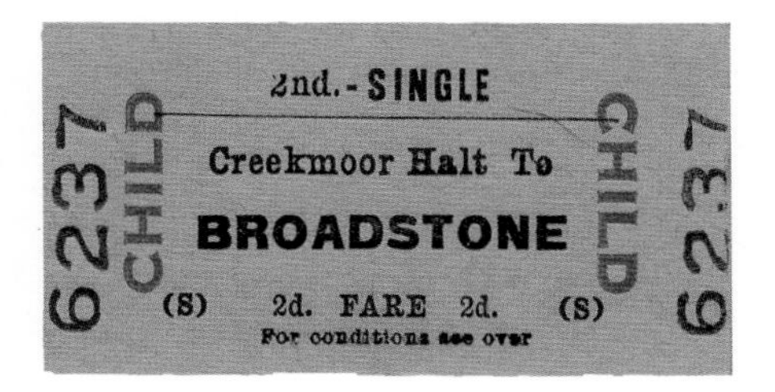

The circuitous Brockenhurst to Broadstone line was originally part of the 60½ miles-long line between Southampton and Dorchester, via Ringwood and Wimborne, which was spearheaded by Mr. A. L. Castleman, an energetic Wimborne solicitor, and was consequently known as 'Castleman's Corkscrew'. It was opened on 1st June 1847, at a time when towns like Ringwood and Wimborne were relatively large centres and Bournemouth had yet to develop. When the 'main line' from London to Bournemouth was opened throughout the 'Corkscrew' lost much of its importance and faded into obscurity with a meagre service of half a dozen weekday trains in each direction, plus a token service of two trains on Sundays. The route was clearly unremunerative and tabled for closure in the Beeching Report of 1963, and this was implemented from 4th May 1964. Not surprisingly, the line was hardly a Mecca for railway photographers and few colour pictures appear to have been taken, but here is a shot of an unidentified Ivatt Class 2MT 2-6-2T hauling the two-coach 2.26pm Bournemouth to Brockenhurst train near Ringwood on 27th September 1963. *Martin Smith*

The 2.04pm Bournemouth West to Brockenhurst train, with M7 Class 0-4-4T No.30379 in charge, crosses the river Stour at Wimborne on 7th September 1962. The train's passenger accommodation is composed of a two-coach set of Maunsell stock equipped for 'pull-push' working. Note the superb cloud formation in the background. *John Beckett*

Pictures taken on the Weymouth Quay tramway are always immediately recognisable because they are an amazing jumble of a train with boats and cars and, in this case, a public house! The history of the line can be traced back to October 1865 when it opened for horse-drawn goods traffic; the line was a joint venture involving both the Great Western Railway (GWR) and LSWR. The ensuing years witnessed gradual improvements but regular passenger workings did not commence until 1889 after widening of the town bridge and the completion of a new landing stage. This meant that boat passengers had the convenience of a through train and would no longer have to make their own way from the station to the quay. The tramway's heyday was probably during the 1950s when as many as eight boat trains were scheduled on summer Saturdays with two or three during the night; goods traffic was also buoyant. The inevitable decline of the tramway started in the 1960s as private motoring became the norm for the masses and the line was closed to regular traffic from 26th September 1987. Unfortunately the cramped layout of the terminal thwarted its development for container traffic. Despite its short length the tramway was probably one of the most difficult lines to operate in the country, solely due to reasons outside the railway's control. Parked cars often blocked the line and had to be removed before a train could pass, also, if that wasn't enough for the hard pressed staff to deal with, flooding was a problem at one point on the line due to high tides. In this picture 1366 Class 0-6-0PT locomotive No.1369 is seen proceeding gingerly towards the quay with a boat train in tow on 3rd September 1961. Note the gentleman standing on the footplate steps; he is presumably the flagman. Every train had to carry a flagman in compliance with an Act of Parliament passed in the 1880s.
John Beckett

The local people in the Swanage area were hostile to the idea of a railway linking their town to the national system and various proposals were strenuously opposed by local residents. The first scheme, mooted in 1847, came to nothing and, after a very long wait, an Act of Parliament was eventually obtained by the promoters and this received the Royal Assent on 18th July 1881. The line opened for passenger traffic on 20th May 1885. Ironically when closure was planned the local people strenuously opposed that proposal too! The opposition to closure, which occurred in 1972, resulted in the formation of a preservation society and today the Swanage Railway is one of Dorset's foremost tourist attractions and brings thousands of visitors to the town. Apart from the outstanding Dorset countryside through which the line passes, many buildings on the Wareham to Swanage line were constructed using the local Purbeck stone and these give the branch a special character all of its own. A hint of the lovely landscape in this glorious part of the world can be seen in this picture of M7 Class 0-4-4T No.30111 leaving Corfe Castle station with a train towards Wareham on 9th September 1962. This shot was taken from the mound on which stands Corfe Castle, an ancient ruin that dominates the village.
John Beckett

The train pictured in the previous photograph is seen earlier in the day, this time with No.30111 propelling towards Swanage. This portrait was taken south of Corfe Castle station. Quite an intensive service was operated on the Swanage branch in BR days and Corfe Castle station was regularly used to pass trains on the single line. The station there is one of the most attractive preserved stations in Great Britain and is situated in a quiet location, well away from the busy main road that passes thorough the village. In times gone by two Pullman cars converted for use as camping coaches were sited here, amid delightful surrounding countryside, and were also within relatively easy reach of the sea. *John Beckett*

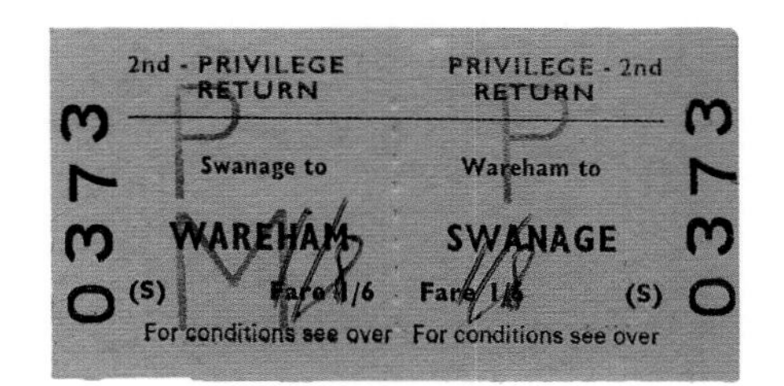

In September 1966 diesel multiple units replaced steam traction on the Swanage branch and from that time the only steam-hauled passenger workings seen on the line were rail tours specially arranged for enthusiasts. The LCGB's 'Dorset Coast Express', which started in London, visited the branch on 7th May 1967 and employed Bulleid Pacific No.34023 *Blackmore Vale* as principal motive power on the branch, assisted by a BR Standard 2-6-4T locomotive at the other end of the train on one trip and a BR Standard 2-6-0 on the other run. By this date it was known that steam on the 'Southern' only had two more months to live and there were tours virtually every weekend – obviously a trip down the usually diesel-worked Swanage branch was an added attraction. Here the cavalcade is seen climbing away from Corfe Castle towards Swanage on a rather gloomy day, with Nine Barrow Down providing the backdrop. Note the train includes coaches in BR's new corporate blue and grey livery. *John Beckett*

Many of the buildings on the Swanage branch were built using the local stone of which the small engine shed at Swanage is a typical example; it has a pitched slate roof. The shed was constructed by the LSWR when the line opened in 1885 and was on a rather restricted site; locomotives could not enter without operation of the 50-feet diameter turntable. Originally the building possessed an arched entrance but in about 1958 an M7 Class engine collided with the structure and a simple lintel was installed. In this illustration a rather dirty Ivatt-designed Class 2MT 2-6-2T, No.41230, is seen passing the shed with a three-coach train from Wareham on 20th August 1966. The shed was closed when diesels took over a few weeks after this scene was recorded but, fortunately, the building survived and is now a constant hive of activity as it is used by the Swanage Railway's locomotive department. *Roy Hobbs*

Purists would no doubt contend with considerable justification that the Weymouth to Yeovil line, which was opened throughout by the GWR in 1857, has no place in an album about SR branch lines. Whilst it is true that this stretch of line was really GWR territory it came under SR control for a time in the 1950s, and SR locomotives based at Weymouth regularly worked over the Yeovil line. Yeovil Town station however was originally the terminus of the Salisbury & Yeovil Railway. The route gained a place in the history books when three tomato trains were routed this way on the very last day of SR steam – probably the highest concentration of SR steam on that fateful day! In this illustration, taken on 9th July 1967, the last day of SR steam, the 3.00pm Weymouth to Westbury train of 'perishable produce' (actually tomatoes from the Channel Islands) is depicted steaming away from Maiden Newton with BR Standard Class 5MT No.73092 in command. The line visible in the left foreground is the erstwhile branch to Bridport which was closed in 1975. *John Beckett*

Opposite A Dorset panorama. One can only imagine the deafening blast being produced by Stanier Class 5MT 4-6-0 No.45493 as it assists Bulleid 'West Country' Pacific No.34100 *Appledore* up the formidable 1 in 51 gradient towards Evershot tunnel on 3rd July 1966. The volume of noise from No.45493 probably ensured that *Appledore*'s softer three-cylinder exhaust beat was inaudible. The pair were hauling the LCGB's 'Green Arrow' rail tour and the train, as the title suggests, had been booked for V2 Class 2-6-2 No.60919 which had been brought down from Dundee especially for this tour. The V2 was in a delicate state of health, however, and the long journey to Nine Elms shed had taken its toll with the result that it was declared unfit to work the train, and SR motive power had to be substituted. The SR operating authorities patched up the V2 and had planned to use it on the tour later in the day so that the participants were not entirely disappointed; with this in mind it was despatched to Eastleigh, but on arrival there an injector was found to be faulty and the plan was abandoned. No.60919 was sent back towards London but suffered a hot box *en route* at Basingstoke and retired to the shed where at least it was visible when the rail tour passed hauled by Bulleid 'Pacific' No.34002 *Salisbury* – how frustrating! *John Beckett*

A 'Battle of Britain' Class Pacific in quite respectable external condition, No.34078, 222 *Squadron,* simmers at Yeovil Town station in the summer of 1963. The first railway in the Yeovil area was the Bristol & Exeter Railway's (B&ER) broad gauge branch from Taunton which opened to Hendford, on the western fringe of the town, in October 1853. When the Frome to Yeovil (Pen Mill) line was opened on 1st September 1856 the line from Taunton was extended, thus enabling the two routes to be linked. For a short period LSWR trains from Sherborne ran into Hendford station using a spur line from Bradford Abbas. Construction of Yeovil Town station was a joint venture between the B&ER and the LSWR and it opened on 1st June 1861, on which date the LSWR branch from Yeovil Junction station also opened for business. Yeovil Town station had a fine frontage and originally possessed a lofty train shed, but this was replaced by standard 'Southern' platform canopies in the 1930s. The station's decline was rapid, beginning with the closure of the predominantly rural line to Taunton in June 1964. The last goods workings ran in 1968, and the station's final role was merely as a reception area for track components lifted during the singling of the Castle Cary to Dorchester route. In 1970 the local authority sanctioned demolition of the imposing station building and Yeovil Town station, which had been by far the most conveniently sited station in the town, was erased from the landscape. It should be noted that the line from Sherborne was originally part of the Salisbury & Yeovil Railway which was worked by the LSWR; it was taken over by that company in 1878. *Derek Penney*

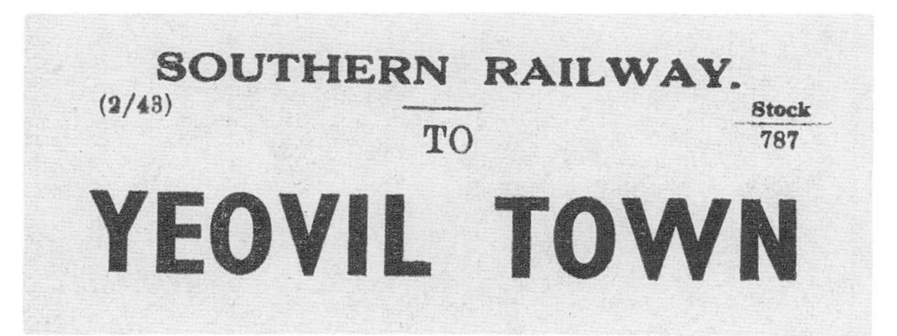
SOUTHERN RAILWAY.
(2/43) TO Stock 787
YEOVIL TOWN

A general view of Yeovil Town station and locomotive shed taken on 11th July 1964. By the date of this photograph the line to Taunton had been closed and Yeovil Town station was served only by shuttle services to both the Pen Mill and Junction stations; the former lasted until 29th November 1965 while services to Yeovil Junction survived until 3rd October 1966, from which date they were diverted to Pen Mill station and Yeovil Town was closed completely. The three-road, brick-built engine shed had arched entrances and a slated, pitched roof, and probably dated from the coming of the Salisbury & Yeovil Railway in 1861. There was a coal stage on the station side of the yard but the very short turntable was removed as long ago as 1917, most engines making use of the much longer turntable available at Yeovil Junction. In the mid-1950s a selection of SR classes could be found at the shed, including U Class 'Moguls', T9 4-4-0s and M7 plus O2 tank classes. At this time the GWR classes based in the Yeovil area were accommodated at Pen Mill shed, but when this establishment closed in early 1959 these engines migrated to the 'Southern' shed which took on a more cosmopolitan atmosphere. The shed was closed in June 1965 and the site converted to a car park. *Michael Chown*

A view of Lyme Regis station, thought to have been taken on (what appears to be) a glorious summer's day in the late 1950s, with the rolling hills of Dorset just visible on the horizon. Note that the signal in the distance, adjacent to the tiny locomotive shed, is in the 'off' position, so presumably a down train was expected. Movements at the station were controlled by the 14-lever wooden signal box seen in the middle of the picture. The milk churns on the platform may have been in use for their usual purpose, but churns were also used to convey water for domestic use from Lyme Regis to the intermediate station of Combpyne. Lyme Regis station had only one platform face with a run-round loop, but the bay platform, on the left, could accommodate a few vehicles and the coach seen here was no doubt used for strengthening purposes at busy times. Steam traction ended in November 1963, but steam returned for a brief period in early 1965 due to a shortage of diesel units. Unfortunately, Lyme Regis station was inconveniently located around 250ft above the town and this may have been a factor in its closure, local bus services no doubt being more convenient for travellers without their own cars. The line was relatively busy in the brief summer holiday period but quiet in the wintertime and the inevitable closure occurred from 29th November 1965 – a sad day. *Stuart Ackley collection*

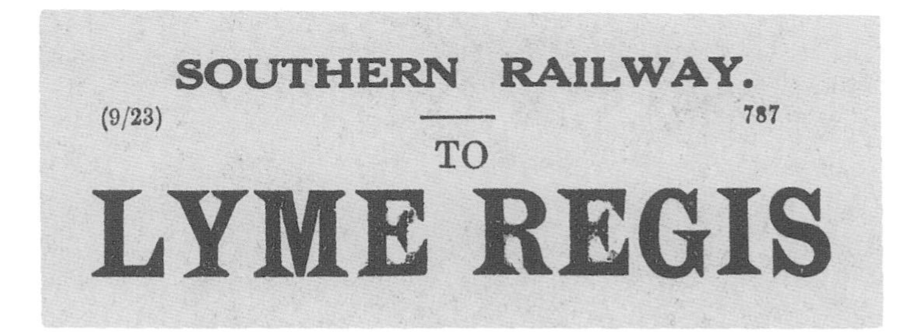

Parliamentary approval for the construction of the 6¾ miles-long branch from Axminster to Lyme Regis was given in 1871 to a local concern and the first sod was cut on 29th September 1874, an event that was apparently marked by a local public holiday. Sadly, the local company rapidly ran out of money and the parliamentary powers lapsed in 1876. Many years later, on 15th June 1899, the Light Railway Commissioners granted powers for the building of a light railway and work began on 19th June 1900. The difficult terrain and bad weather delayed opening until 24th August 1903. Like many light railways the Lyme Regis branch was characterised by steep gradients and very tight curves, the principal civil engineering work being the ten-arch Cannington viaduct, built by 'Concrete Bob' McAlpine, which is 203 yards-long and 93ft high; being a listed structure it still strides across the valley today. The very heavy inclines on the Lyme Regis branch can be judged by the fact that the viaduct is approached from Axminster on a 1 in 40 falling gradient which eased to 1 in 82 on the viaduct. In this view of Lyme Regis station taken on 8th July 1959, Adams 'Radial' tank locomotive No.30584 is depicted running in to the station with a train from Axminster. These delightful engines lasted until early 1961 when they were replaced by Ivatt-designed 2-6-2Ts that were passed to work the branch following the easing of many tight curves. The Bulleid coaches in the bay on the left had presumably formed a through portion of a train from Waterloo which operated regularly on summer Saturdays only. At the time of this picture there were around nine trains each way on the branch on weekdays. *R. C. Riley*

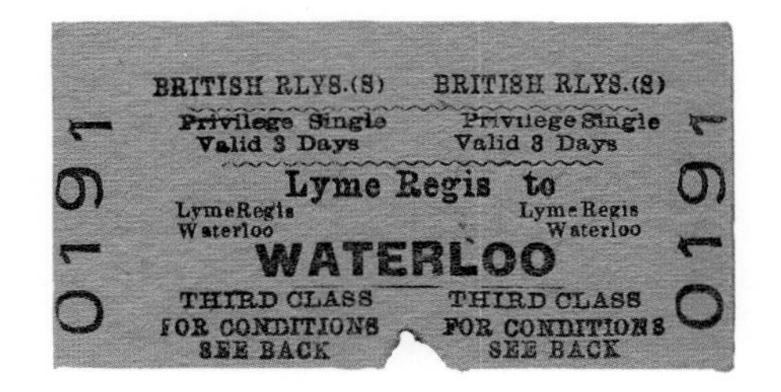

41307

During the last years of the S&D BR Standard Class 4MT 2-6-4Ts became a regular sight on the line and a pair of these locomotives powered the very last timetabled passenger train over the route. These engines were drafted in following a successful trial run on 4th November 1963 on the 1.10pm Bournemouth to Bath train and 7.05pm return. In this picture No.80059 is seen leaving Evercreech New with a southbound working on a sunny day in July 1965. This machine spent its early years working on the London Midland Region in the London area and was based at Kentish Town and Neasden sheds for a time before moving to the Southern Region in December 1959. *Ian Wright*

Opposite The history of this much-loved line has been well documented over the years so only a brief outline is necessary. The first section of (what later became) the Somerset & Dorset line (S&D) was opened by the Somerset Central Railway (SCR) from Highbridge to Glastonbury on 28th August 1854, and the rest of the route was built on a piecemeal basis during the ensuing twenty years. A major milestone in its development occurred on 3rd February 1862 when the Somerset Central extended its line from Glastonbury to Cole (near Bruton) where it met the Dorset Central Railway's line from Templecombe. The two lines amalgamated later the same year to form the Somerset & Dorset Railway. Through running from Wimborne to Burnham-on-Sea became possible in August 1863. The route did not attract as much traffic as the promoters anticipated and they decided to gamble everything on driving a new line across the Mendip hills to Bath where a junction was made with the mighty Midland Railway; the so-called Bath Extension opened on 20th July 1874. Virtually overnight the fortunes of the S&D were transformed as it became an important link between the North of England, the Midlands and the South Coast. This relative prosperity continued well into the 1950s during which time the line was particularly busy with heavy holiday trains during the summer months, in addition to the considerable goods traffic carried, especially coal at the northern end of the line. However, the decision of the Western Region in 1962 to re-route the holiday trains, and the legendary 'Pines Express' that connected Manchester with Bournemouth, immediately reduced the line's status to little more than that of a country branch and, even worse, many of the S&D's traditional flows of goods traffic were also diverted away. After a slow, lingering decline this once-proud line was finally closed in March 1966 amid much anger and resentment that the authorities had done nothing to reduce costs and stimulate business. An outstandingly beautiful line had been 'sabotaged and defeated'. Photographed in the line's last year of operation, Ivatt Class 2MT 2-6-2T No.41307 scuttles along near Horsington with a Templecombe to Highbridge train on 17th July 1965. *John Beckett*

The S&D had many appealing features, and even some of the place names and stations along the line, such as Shoscombe & Single Hill and Sturminster Newton, conjured up a delightful rural charm. Perhaps the same cannot be said of Cannard's Grave, south of Shepton Mallet, which is the location of a crossroads. Cannard was a criminal who was executed at that spot and the road junction was named after him as a gruesome reminder of that event. In this illustration the LCGB's 'Somerset & Dorset' rail tour is seen plodding uphill near Cannard's Grave with S&D 2-8-0 No.53808 in charge on 30th September 1962. Note that the photographer appears to have been lucky with the sun which is obligingly shining on the locomotive and front three carriages, the rest of the train being in shade. Earlier this train had traversed the Ringwood to Broadstone line and the day ended with a run behind a 'County' Class 4-6-0 from Didcot to Paddington. *John Beckett*

Maximum effort! Class 7F 2-8-0 No.53807 lifts the 10.42am SO Exmouth to Cleethorpes through train up the last few yards to Masbury summit on 25th August 1962. This service conveyed returning holiday-makers from the Devon coast to the Midlands and Lincolnshire area and could also be used by hardy holiday-makers from the Midlands staying at Cleethorpes who were prepared for a very late arrival at the resort. The sets of coaching stock used on these trains were provided by the Eastern and Southern regions and the rake seen here, which includes Maunsell, Bulleid and BR Standard vehicles, hardly requires identification of ownership. What an assortment of carriages! *John Beckett*

The S&D Class 7F 2-8-0s were, as their power classification suggests, designed primarily to work heavy goods traffic over the steep gradients of the Mendip Hills between Bath and Evercreech Junction. The locomotives were noted for their particularly effective brakes when working downhill – a quality that was just as essential as their pulling power when going the other way! Relatively few colour pictures of Class 7Fs working goods traffic were taken, however, because most photographers were only around at week-ends when there was usually very little movement of goods. Here is No.53808 powering the 2.00pm Bath to Evercreech Junction goods; it is approaching Binegar's down distant signal on 12th September 1962. By this date the Western Region administered most of the line and pursued a relentless policy of diverting as much business as possible away from the S&D; this may be reflected in the fairly short train seen here which was a derisory load for one of these immensely strong engines. *John Beckett*

Made in Calcutta? This delightful Saxby & Farmer signal works plate was photographed near Binegar on 25th August 1962. *John Beckett*

A Templecombe to Bath (Green Park) stopping train, with BR Standard 4-6-0 No.75073 in charge, descends towards Chilcompton tunnel on 25th August 1962. The line falls at 1 in 50 at this point from Chilcompton station which is hidden from view at the top of the picture; the village forms the backdrop. Heavy goods trains were frequently banked from Radstock, often by a LMSR 'Jinty' 0-6-0, and the banker was normally detached at Masbury summit which was 811 feet above sea level. Passenger trains were, of course, sometimes double-headed over the Mendips from Bath to Evercreech Junction where a turntable was available. One can only imagine the stirring sight and deafening sound of a train ascending the very heavy gradient at this point. *John Beckett*

Home sweet home. Radstock was the centre of the North Somerset coalfield and had a small depot which was a sub-shed of Bath (Green Park). A number of locomotives were stabled at Radstock for shunting the many coal trains that originated in the area and probably only returned to Bath when a boiler washout was required or, perhaps, a defect needed attention. In this shot an unidentified LMSR 'Jinty' 0-6-0T simmers outside its shed on 16th May 1964. The tiny depot was equipped with an inspection pit, water crane complete with brazier and a rather rudimentary hoist (behind the locomotive) for coaling purposes. Note the rather fine S&D lower quadrant signals on the right. In times gone by there were three collieries in the immediate environs of Radstock so the yards in the town must have been a hive of activity. Radstock shed's most well-known residents were a pair of diminutive Sentinel shunters, built in 1929, which were the only locomotives permitted to pass underneath Tyning's bridge that had a very restricted clearance. Radstock shed remained operational, merely stabling a diesel shunter, until November 1973. *Colour-Rail.com*

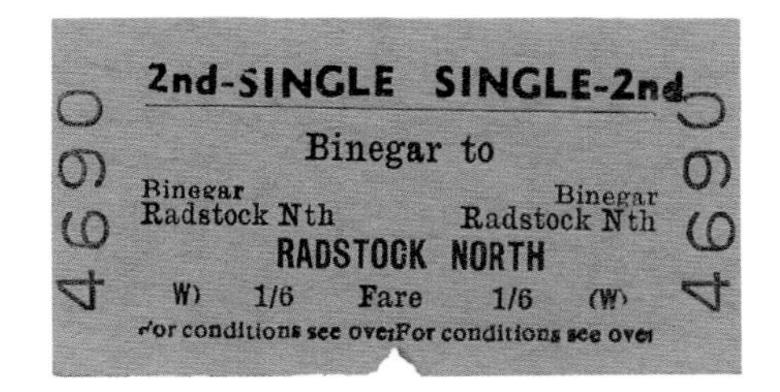

It would be something of an understatement to say that on summer Saturdays the operating authorities on the S&D line were stretched to provide motive power for the many extra trains that operated. Virtually any locomotive that could turn a wheel was pressed into service and sometimes memorable combinations were witnessed. On one occasion a bunker-first 'Jinty' piloted a S&D 2-8-0 that was presumably ailing, while on 11th August 1962 Bulleid 'West Country' Pacific No.34043 *Combe Martin* was seen assisting BR Standard Class 9F No.92245 on the 7.43am SO Bradford to Bournemouth train. Here, the 7.00am SO Cleethorpes to Exmouth is depicted near Wellow with Class 2P No.40634 piloting 4F No.44422 on 9th September 1961. In previous years this train, which was loaded to only ten bogies, would have been powered by a S&D Class 7F as far as Templecombe, but by the date of this picture only five members of this class were serviceable and it was frequently rostered for a Class 4F 0-6-0 and Class 2P 4-4-0 in double harness. The leading engine was one of the 2Ps built especially for use on the S&D at Derby in 1928 and would originally have been finished in its very appealing blue livery. *John Beckett*

The tower of St. Julian's church stands out above the trees as Class 2P No.40700 assists rebuilt Bulleid Pacific No.34028 *Eddystone* past Wellow with the 12.20pm Bournemouth to Nottingham express on 9th September 1961. Wellow station, which is just out of sight around the bend, was one of the best-patronised wayside stations on the line due to the village being situated in a steeply-sided valley that was unsuitable for buses. Consequently, the villagers were hit hard when the line was closed. *John Beckett*

The sun may not be shining but, even so, the scenery looks absolutely glorious as an unidentified Class 4F 0-6-0 takes the 4.15pm Templecombe to Bath (Green Park) stopping train on the last leg of its journey; it was photographed between Midford and Combe Down tunnel on 7th August 1961. The S&D was famous for its fascinating locomotive combinations, some of which could not be seen elsewhere in Great Britain, but here is a different example of the line's cosmopolitan character, a LMSR-designed locomotive hauling a 'Southern', Maunsell-designed 3-set of coaches. *John Beckett*

In complete contrast to the northern section of the S&D line, which had some of the steepest gradients of any line carrying heavy trains in England, the Evercreech Junction to Highbridge line was almost totally flat. The line was, as previously mentioned, originally part of the S&D 'main Line' connecting the Bristol Channel with the English Channel and the promoters envisaged that their line would attract a lot of traffic. Their optimism was never fulfilled, however, and after the Bath extension was opened in 1874 the Highbridge line, and the later extension to Burnham-on-Sea, was downgraded in importance and was subsequently known to S&D staff as 'The Branch'. In addition to being flat, apart from Pylle bank, the Highbridge route was also dead straight for mile after mile and another feature of the line was the number of level crossings over minor by-ways. Owing to their isolated location many of these had no mains water supply and depended on the morning up goods train for deliveries of water in five-gallon milk churns. Traditionally the motive power used on the line was former Midland Railway Class 3F 0-6-0s on goods and Johnson 0-4-4Ts on passenger trains, but in the closing years more-modern Great Western Collett 0-6-0s and Ivatt 2-6-2Ts took over. Here No.3216, one of the former class, is depicted at West Pennard with the 2.20pm Highbridge to Templecombe stopping train on 18th August 1962. This was the nearest crossing place and block post to Evercreech Junction. Unfortunately, the inhabitants of West Pennard had a very long walk to reach their station, the village being two miles distant on the Shepton Mallet to Glastonbury road. *Alan Chandler*

An unmistakable location. Former LSWR O2 Class 0-4-4T No.W35 *Freshwater* accelerates away from Ryde Pier Head station with a train to Ventnor on 28th September 1963. The original pier at Ryde was opened as long ago as July 1814 while the pier tramway, in the foreground, dates from August 1864. The trams were horse-drawn until 1886 from which time they were powered by electricity, petrol-driven vehicles taking over in 1927. The third pier, which was constructed alongside the other two, was jointly owned by the LBSCR/LSWR and carries the tracks from Ryde Esplanade to the Pier Head station where boat connections are made for Portsmouth Harbour. The trains, however, were run by the Isle of Wight Railway (IWR) and the Isle of Wight Central Railway (IWCR) and these companies owned the formation south of Ryde St. John's Road station. The railway pier was remodelled in the 1930s and received Grade Two listed building status in 1976. There was another pier at Ryde at one time, this being built by the Stokes Bay Pier and Railway Company who ran a competing ferry service from the mainland. It was opened in 1864 but fell into disuse after the independent company was taken over by the LSWR and the ferry service terminated. Demolition was authorised in 1916 and by 1920 the pier had, one might say, disappeared. *Les Dench*

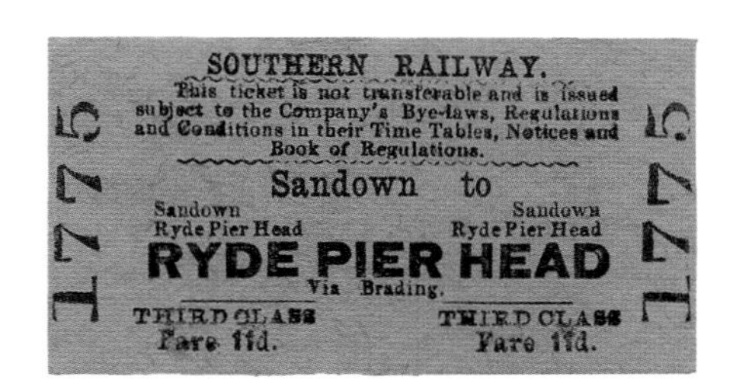

Judging by the direction in which its exhaust smoke is blowing No.W22 *Brading* had to contend with a very strong westerly wind, in addition to its six-coach load, as it passed along the pier hauling a train for the Sandown line on 26th June 1965. Note the Portsmouth ferry berthed at the end of the pier and the mainland visible on the horizon. Actually the term 'mainland' is not wholly accurate because Portsmouth is itself built on an island. The tramway on the left of the shot still had four more years of operation ahead of it when this picture was taken, closing in 1969. *John Beckett*

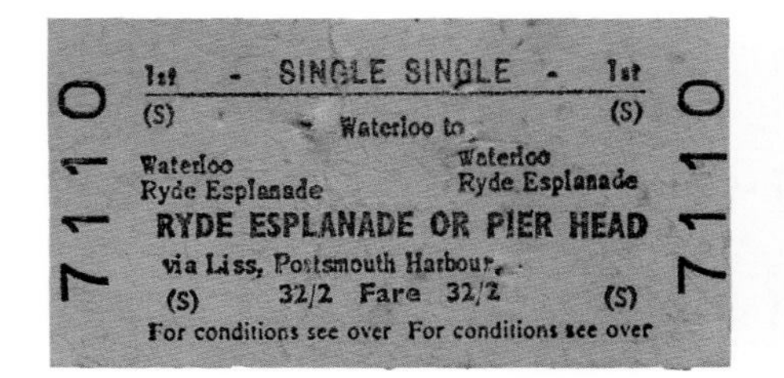

7110
1st - SINGLE SINGLE - 1st
(S) Waterloo to (S)
Waterloo Waterloo
Ryde Esplanade Ryde Esplanade
RYDE ESPLANADE OR PIER HEAD
via Liss, Portsmouth Harbour,
(S) 32/2 Fare 32/2 (S)
For conditions see over For conditions see over
7110

7605
2nd - ORDINARY RETURN
ORD - 2nd
RE URN
CHILD
Ryde Esplanade or Ryde Pier Head to WATERLOO via Portsmouth Harbour and Liss
Waterloo to RYDE ESPLANADE or RYDE PIER HEAD via Liss and Portsmouth Harbour
(S) Fare 22/9 Fare 22/9 (S)
For conditions see over For conditions see over
7605

For many years Newport, from where routes radiated in four directions, could justly claim to have been the operational hub of the Isle of Wight system but most of those lines were rural in nature and carried insufficient traffic to justify their long-term survival. By 1965 only the Ryde to Ventnor/Cowes routes remained and Ryde St. John's Road station and its adjacent works and shed had become the operational nerve centre of the island. Here, no fewer than four locomotives are on view, the two behind the signal box are actually on the shed, while the engine on the right of the picture, No.W32 *Bonchurch,* is 'dead' outside the works having been withdrawn from traffic for almost a year and is no doubt awaiting scrap. No.W17 *Seaview,* however, was still very much in service and appears to be pulling away with a Ventnor line train. The large signal box possessed a 45-lever frame and was previously located at Waterloo East. The picture was taken on 4th September 1965. *Les Dench*

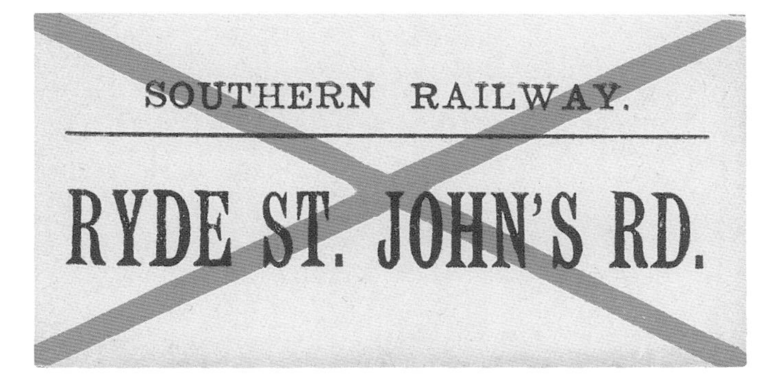

No.W32 *Bonchurch* is depicted apparently waiting to leave Ryde shed with what can only be described as a truly vintage coal train – note the really ancient brake van. Judging by the headcode it appears to be destined for Ventnor where supplies of coal were kept. *Derek Penney*

9174

2nd - SINGLE   SINGLE - 2nd

Ryde Pier Head to

Ryde Pier Head   Ryde Pier Head

Ryde St. J. Rd.   Ryde St. J. Rd.

RYDE ST. JOHNS ROAD

by TRAIN ONLY

(S)   4d. FARE 4d.   (S)

For conditions see over   For conditions see over

9174

Two spotlessly clean O2 Class locomotives present a fine sight as they await their next turn of duty outside Ryde shed on 24th April 1962. At that time the engines on the Isle of Wight system were always kept in exemplary condition as illustrated here. Amazingly, the shed depicted was actually the third engine shed to be built at Ryde. The first shed was a two-road building that was subsequently incorporated into the works, a replacement shed constructed of corrugated iron being built by the IWR in 1874. In 1930 this crude structure was itself replaced by the building seen here which could hold eight of the O2 Class tank locomotives. It was built using asbestos on a steel framework and it is thought that some of the girders were redundant LBSCR electrification gantries; a new, large coal stage was also provided. *Derek Penney*

Well, there is certainly no shortage of luggage space on this train – the author has no idea why this was out of all proportion to the passenger accommodation provided. Perhaps there was a meeting of pigeon fanciers and space was needed for pigeon baskets, or possibly there was a bonny baby competition being held somewhere on the island, hence additional room was required for prams! Actually, the vehicle formed immediately behind the locomotive is of particular interest, being a full brake coach specially converted from a former passenger-carrying carriage. The identity of this particular vehicle is not known, but it is likely it began life as a SECR 'Birdcage' brake and was shipped over to the island in the late 1940s. In 1956 four coaches were selected for conversion to full brakes but during the course of this work most of their character was lost, the body being encased in steel sheeting. The guard's position at one end of the vehicle was retained together with end look-out windows. This intriguing shot was taken in April 1962 and depicts No.W24 *Calbourne* coming into Ryde St. John's Road. *Derek Penney*

The railway system on the Isle of Wight was an irresistible draw for railway aficionados and, looking at this image of O2 Class No.W24 *Calbourne* leaving Ryde with a Ventnor line train in April 1962, it is not difficult to see why it was such an attraction. The last O2 Class engines on the mainland were withdrawn during 1962 and, by the end of the same year, pre-grouping coaching stock on the mainland had also become a thing of the past, apart from one or two oddities such as the Lancing workmen's train which lasted another year or so. Thus, during the final few years of its existence the pre-grouping scene on the island attracted many visitors who came to experience the last vintage, standard gauge steam-hauled trains working on the national system. *Derek Penney*

The evening sunshine beautifully illuminates O2 Class No.W30 *Shorwell* as it hurries along between St. John's Road station and Smallbrook Junction with the 7.25pm Ryde Pier Head to Ventnor on 16th June 1964. The Ventnor line was originally proposed by the Isle of Wight Railway and by 1864 it had reached Shanklin; the final section on to Ventnor was opened two years later. *Michael Chown*

The track layout immediately identifies the location of this photograph, Smallbrook Junction, which was, at least during the peak summer period, a very busy spot indeed. In this April 1962 picture No.W36 *Carisbrooke* is seen approaching the tiny signal box which was positioned between the two running lines; the photographer was presumably standing on the signal box steps. Note that there are no signal arms on the bracket signal visible in the background and the connection from the down track to the single line to Cowes, on the left, appears to be covered with a thick coating of rust indicating that during the winter months the railway between Ryde St. John's Road station and Smallbrook was operated as two separate single lines. The first signalman on duty after the long winter period would certainly have needed a can of oil and a duster! *Derek Penney*

The evening sun highlights O2 Class locomotive No.W16 *Ventnor* as it climbs away from Wroxall with a Ryde to Ventnor working on 6th June 1965. Wroxall station was opened in November 1866 and closed from 18th April 1966, so it just missed its centenary. When the Ryde to Ventnor line was originally proposed it was intended to route it via Luccombe and Bonchurch but objections from local landowners forced the IWR to alter the route in favour of Wroxall. This detour involved a steep climb from Shanklin over Apse bank, which no doubt proved a challenge to generations of footplatemen and, even worse, the construction of a long tunnel under St. Boniface Down. *Alan Reeve*

The fireman is apparently checking the water level in the side tank of No.W28 *Ashey* as it prepares to run round its train at Ventnor on 22nd May 1964. This view of a locomotive in the shunting neck at Ventnor station before running round was taken by most enthusiasts who made the pilgrimage to the Isle of Wight. How many stations offered such a magnificent background, the view being made even more interesting by the old Southern Railway sign above the station entrance? It is sometimes forgotten that for many years there was another station in the town, Ventnor West (formerly Ventnor Town), this being at the end of a branch from Merstone; it was originally built by the Isle of Wight Central Railway and opened in 1900. Apart from Ventnor itself, the line served only a few small villages and closed as long ago as 15th September 1952. *Alan Reeve*

After threading the 1,312 yards-long single-bore tunnel under St. Boniface Down, which rises to over 700ft., trains suddenly emerged into daylight and came to a halt in Ventnor station, where the raucous cry of sea birds circling above and salty sea air were in distinct contrast to the dark and smoky confines of the tunnel. Note the very restricted layout where trains plunged into the tunnel almost immediately after leaving the station. No.W20 *Shanklin,* in really sparkling condition, is seen running round its train on 27th September 1963. *Les Dench*

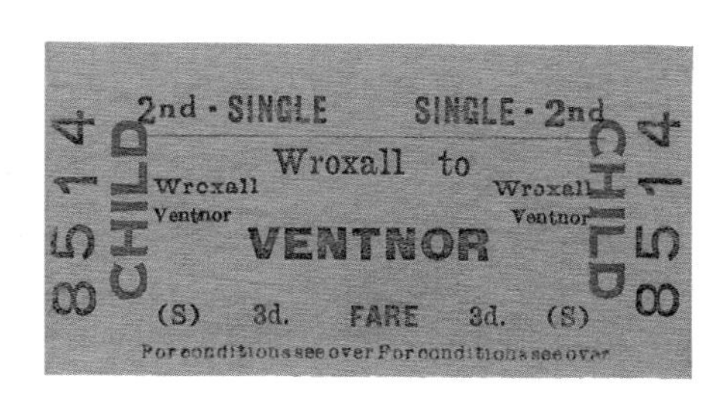

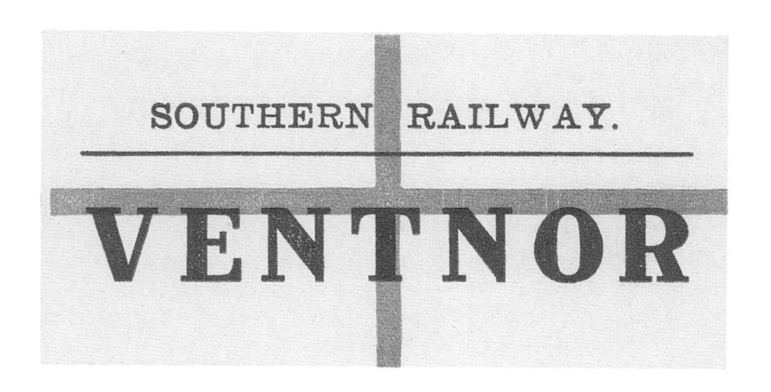

A seagull's-eye view. Ventnor station was undoubtedly situated in a distinctive and memorable location, 276ft. above sea level and surrounded on three sides by high chalk downland, part of which was tree-covered. The steep walk down to the sea, not to mention the walk back up the hill to the station, also no doubt made the journey to Ventnor memorable for other reasons. Here, No.W17 *Seaview* 'blows off' in Ventnor station before leaving with a train to Ryde on 16th September 1961. Note the caves in the rock face – one wonders if they were inhabited! It is thought, however that the caves were used by a local coal merchant for storage. *John Beckett*

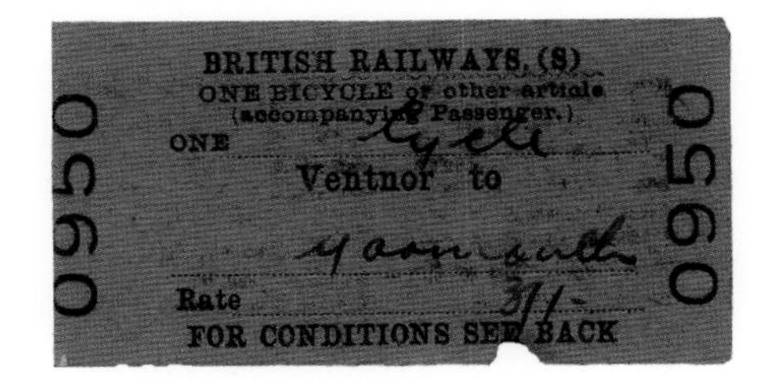

Strangely, the first section of the Ryde to Cowes line to be opened was that north of Newport which was brought into use by the Cowes & Newport Railway (CNR) in 1862, two years before the Ryde to Shanklin section opened. The CNR operated in splendid isolation for 13 years before it joined the rest of the island railway system, when the Ryde & Newport Railway commenced operations in 1875. Compared to the Shanklin line, the Cowes route is much more rural in nature and in this picture O2 Class No.W14 *Fishbourne* is seen restarting a Ryde to Cowes train away from Ashey station on 3rd April 1965. Incredibly, there used to be a racecourse at Ashey, but its career was abruptly terminated by a fire that wrecked the grandstand in the late 1920s. The original station building, on the left, is still in existence at the time of writing as a private residence but trains on the Isle of Wight Steam Railway serve only the former down platform. This platform was disused for many years but was restored to use in the early 1960s when there was ground movement and BR were obliged to slew the track to the position formerly occupied by the down line. *John Beckett*

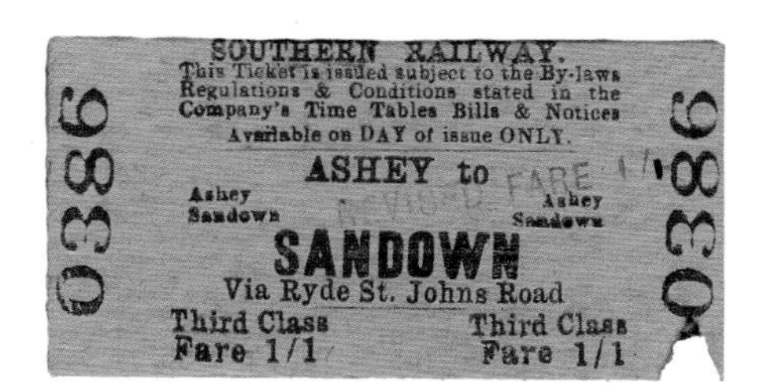

Perhaps the swans can be forgiven for not noticing the train rumbling overhead but the young lads standing on the quay are also guilty of ignoring it! Shame on you! Clearly they could not have been aware that such sights would soon to be just a memory at Newport, the line closing in April 1966 just ten months after this shot was taken of No.W26 *Whitwell* crossing the river Medina with a Cowes to Ryde train on 5th June 1965. What a good spot for a railway picture; there is a really attractive bridge across the river, the Model Stores with its road services to and from the mainland on the left, while tucked away on the extreme right is (what appears to be) a timber yard. Then there are the reflections on the river and various boats to add further interest. One could almost say a train would be a distraction..... *Alan Reeve*

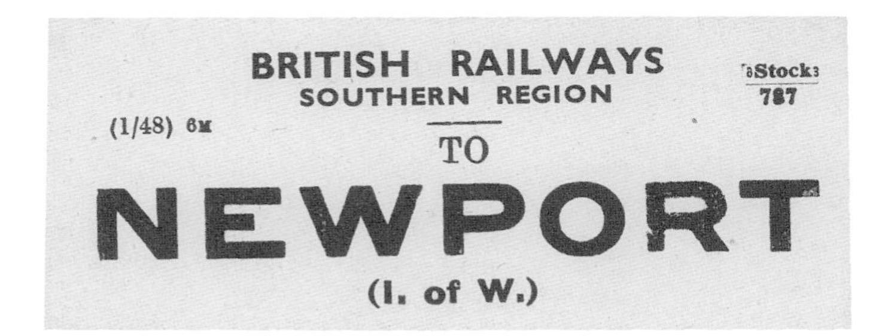

Newport, the county town of the Isle of Wight, was (as previously stated) once the focal point of the island's railway system, upon which no fewer than four routes converged. In the 1930s the lines to both Sandown and Freshwater had quite a reasonable service, there being nine trains on weekdays advertised in the 1933 timetable to Sandown with eight to Freshwater. Due to the short distances involved both lines were vulnerable to road competition and the Freshwater line was the first to go, passenger services being withdrawn from 21st September 1953; the Sandown route followed on 6th February 1956. Ten years later the Ryde to Cowes line closed and Newport was erased from the railway map. This undated illustration, which was presumably taken from a signal or footbridge, gives a good idea of the extent of the railway infrastructure in the town, with the engine shed prominent. The shed was built in the late 1870s when the lines from Merstone and Ryde were completed, and was constructed of wood with corrugated sheeting; consisting of two roads it had a pitched roof with a central raised smoke vent. There was a water tank built over one of the roads, this being clearly visible in the picture. The shed was used for carriage and wagon repairs in addition to light repairs of locomotives. The building beyond the shed was also an engine repair shed at one time but this was converted for carriage painting in 1929. The engine shed was officially closed in November 1957. Note the locomotive standing just in front of the hoist; this is LBSCR E1 Class No.W4 *Wroxall,* a Brighton works product dating from November 1878. In the early 1950s there was a total of four of these engines based at Newport and No.4 survived to become the last member of its class on the island, lasting until November 1960. *Stuart Ackley collection*

The ancient wooden-bodied wagon, rather peculiar water crane with its accompanying brazier, 'Southern' signal, 'South Western' concrete running-in board and delightful little signal box – this gem of a photograph encapsulates why the Isle of Wight lines had such universal appeal. The location is immediately apparent from the picture. This photograph was taken in June 1963, by which time the West Coast Main Line was being electrified and BR's modernisation plan was in full swing. Sadly, modernisation never came to this outpost of the Isle of Wight system and the line from Ryde was closed in April 1966. The infrastructure seen here was not Cowes's only attraction for railway enthusiasts, and it was great fun to witness a locomotive running round its train, a procedure that was carried out in a somewhat unconventional fashion. After the passengers had left the train the engine would be uncoupled and push the carriages back beyond the points. The locomotive would then proceed to the buffers and run-round while the coaches set back into the platform under gravity. One wonders what would have happened if the Chief Operating Officer from Waterloo just happened to be taking a holiday in the Cowes area and witnessed this manoeuvre while waiting for a train...... *Colour-Rail.com*

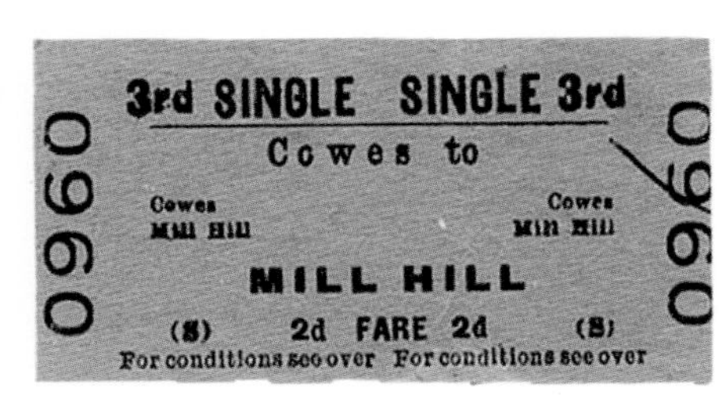

The Brading Harbour Improvements & Railway Co. obtained powers to build the 2½ miles-long branch from Brading to Bembridge in 1874 but construction was slow due to the fact that the line had to cross a large area of marshland. The branch eventually opened to traffic on 27th May 1882 and was operated from the outset by the Isle of Wight Railway who bought the line, reportedly for £430, and took over from 2nd August 1898. There was one intermediate station, at St. Helens, which was a small village on the opposite side of Bembridge harbour to the town. In the 1933 timetable a generous service to and from Brading is advertised, but it can be reasonably assumed that most passengers from Bembridge would be heading for Ryde and the local bus no doubt provided a much more convenient, and possibly cheaper, means of getting there. The branch simply withered away and was an early closure casualty, services being withdrawn from 21st September 1953, the same day that the Freshwater branch succumbed. Unlike at some locations where they acted with almost indecent haste, BR were not in a hurry to demolish the station, a task that was unlikely to have been high on the priorities of the estate department at Waterloo, and the station building was still standing on 17th May 1960 when this picture was taken. Perhaps it was in use as a private residence – who knows? *Stuart Ackley collection*

The ruins at Merstone. Much of the Isle of Wight's population is concentrated on the eastern side of the island and, with the exception of Newport, the county town and administrative centre, much of the interior is made up of quiet, and extremely pleasant, countryside dotted with farms and smallholdings. Note the apparent lack of surrounding habitation in this shot. Despite the unpromising prospects, the Isle of Wight (Newport Junction) Railway opened its line from Sandown to Newport via Merstone in 1875, and in 1897 the Newport, Godshill & St. Lawrence Railway optimistically opened from Merstone to St. Lawrence, near Ventnor. Three years later an extension from St. Lawrence to Ventnor Town station (later West) was brought into use. The latter line must have been totally unremunerative, the 1933 timetable listing a meagre service of only six weekday trains in each direction, and it had the dubious honour of being the first of the island's lines to close, this occurring on 15th September 1952. The Newport to Sandown stretch at least had the benefit of relatively major population centres at each end of the line and this survived until 6th February 1956. In this picture of Merstone station, taken on 8th May 1960, a group of enthusiasts must have felt a sense of despair as they surveyed the scene of total decay and dereliction. The track had only recently been lifted and the chairs lay along the platform edge while the rails and sleepers are still lying around, presumably awaiting removal by the contractor. Regrettably, this was the fate shared by many branch lines in the southern counties.......... *Stuart Ackley collection*